the
Homeschooler's
Guide to ...

OTHER BOOKS BY VICKI CARUANA

Apples & Chalkdust
(Honor Books, 1998)

Success in School
(Focus Publishing, 2000)

Apples & Chalkdust for Teachers
(Honor Books, 2000)

The ABCs of Homeschooling
(Crossway Books, 2001)

Apples & Chalkdust #2
(River Oak Publishing, 2001)

The Organized Homeschooler
(Crossway Books, 2001)

Educating Your Gifted Child
(Crossway Books, 2002)

Prayers from a Teacher's Heart
(River Oak Publishing, 2002)

the Homeschooler's Guide to . . .

TESTING AND EVALUATION
HOME-BASED BUSINESSES
COMMUNITY INVOLVEMENT
HIGH SCHOOL AND COLLEGE ENTRANCE
TRADITIONAL SCHOOLS
HOMESCHOOLING IN THE MILITARY
SUPPORT GROUPS AND CO-OPS
CHILDREN WITH SPECIAL NEEDS
STUDY SKILLS
MUSIC EDUCATION

Vicki Caruana

CROSSWAY BOOKS

A DIVISION OF
GOOD NEWS PUBLISHERS
WHEATON, ILLINOIS

The author is represented by Alive Communications, Inc., 7680 Goddard Street, Suite 200, Colorado Springs, CO 80920.

Library of Congress Cataloging-in-Publication Data
Caruana, Vicki.
    The homeschooler's guide to . . . / Vicki Caruana.
      p. cm.
    Includes bibliographical references and index.
    ISBN 1-58134-357-4 (alk. paper)
    1. Home schooling—Handbooks, manuals, etc. I. Title.
LC40 .C377   2003
371.04'2—dc21   2002154143

BP		13	12	11	10	09	08	07	06	05	04	03
15	14	13	12	11	10	9	8	7	6	5	4	3	2	1

*To my husband Chip
and our children,
Christopher and Charles,*

who support me every step of the way

CONTENTS

ACKNOWLEDGMENTS

I would like to thank those experts who added their words to mine.

Ellyn Davis, of The Elijah Company, an experienced homeschool parent and a successful business owner, offers readers a realistic view of running a home-based business.

Ellie Kay, former homeschool mom of five and a military mom, encourages military homeschoolers that this too is in service to our country.

Shari Henry, editor and columnist in *Homeschooling Today* magazine and author of *Homeschooling: The Middle Years: Your Complete Guide to Successfully Homeschooling the 8- to 12-Year-Old Child*, encourages readers from her own experiences with her children.

Lindsey O'Connor currently homeschools four of her children, including one son with special needs. We are grateful that she allows readers to see her family close-up and personal in her writing.

Laurinda Curti, homeschool mom and music instructor, shares with readers her heart for music and encourages us to step out of our comfort zone and provide the gift of music to our children.

ABOUT THE CONTRIBUTORS

All of the contributors to this book are available to speak to your homeschool group.

Vicki Caruana is the author of *The ABCs of Homeschooling* (2001), *The Organized Homeschooler* (2001), and *Educating Your Gifted Child* (2002), all three published by Crossway Books. She also authored the bestselling book *Apples & Chalkdust* (Honor, 1998) and several other books. She is a popular homeschool writer and speaker. Vicki's mission is to educate and encourage kids and those who live and work with them to strive for excellence. Contact Vicki when you plan your next homeschooling conference or event at vicki@applesandchalkdust.com.

Ellyn Davis: The Elijah Company is really the Davis family. Chris (Dad) grew up in Los Angeles and moved to the Southeast at fifteen when his mother died. (His father had died when Chris was a toddler.) Chris attended the University of Georgia and received a B.A. in business administration and for years owned a construction equipment rental business. Ellyn (Mom) grew up in Atlanta, attended Georgia State and Emory Universities, earned a B.S. and M.S., and completed all but the dissertation for her Ph.D. in microbiology/biochemistry. After Chris and Ellyn married, they both became committed Christians. God eventually led Chris to sell his business, earn a Master's degree in counseling, and become a pastor. You can contact Ellyn at elijahco@elijahco.com.

Homeschooling veteran **Shari Henry** walks parents through the seemingly daunting task of preparing homeschooled children for high school and college. She goes over various high school options. Parents are encouraged to take a realistic look at the options and to weigh pros and cons before getting too far along into the high school years. Curriculum, socialization, internships and career options, and college entrance exams and applications are among the areas covered.

Shari Henry and her husband, Tim Jones, are the homeschooling parents of three children, ages ten to seventeen. She is the former senior editor of *Homeschooling Today* magazine, and the author of *Homeschooling: The Middle Years* (Prima, 1999). You can contact Shari at ShariHenry@aol.com.

Ellie Kay is a military wife who homeschooled five of her seven children for seven years in five different states. She's also a best-selling financial author, national radio commentator for "Money Matters," and a regular guest on CNBC's "Power Lunch." As a "mom on the move," Ellie shares smart ways for military families to homeschool their children and provide continuity in an oftentimes stressful environment. She's an expert in handling the questions that military moms have about moving, location, handling spousal military separations, and how to plug into a homeschool community in a new location. You can contact Ellie at ellie@elliekay.com.

Lindsey O'Connor will teach you, tickle you, and testify of the joy and richness in life with Christ. With warmth and enthusiasm, this mother of four shares from the heart, the trenches, and the Word of God. Her audiences have no problem keeping their eyes open while she's opening their eyes to see the joy and purpose that's ours as we grow close to the Lord. She is a speaker, author, and occasional broadcaster, having anchored television news, produced commercials, and co-hosted and guest-hosted radio programs and was the first female news anchor for the *USA Radio Network*. She is also known for her books—*If Momma Ain't Happy, Ain't Nobody Happy* and *The Christian's Guide to Working from Home*, both from Harvest House. She is equally at home on the platform, in the studio, or at the kitchen sink. Lindsey homeschools three of her five children, including one special needs son. You can contact Lindsey at Lindsey@LindseyO'Connor.com.

Laurinda Curti is a licensed Kindermusik Educator. She has taught homeschool students, ages five through twelve, and general music classes as part of High Country Enrichment Classes at New Life Church in Colorado Springs, Colorado. She is in her fourth year of running her private piano studio where she specializes in foundational music skills. Laurinda emphasizes the importance of music not only for the value of music, but for eternal value in the Kingdom of God. She offers practical suggestions for making music part of the homeschool environment. Laurinda and her husband, George, have four children and reside in Colorado Springs, Colorado. She currently homeschools three of her children, and they are all actively pursuing musical training. You can contact Laurinda at curtimusicmakers@aol.com.

Introduction

Homeschooling is a journey, and on that journey there are always decisions to make. Which curriculum should I use? What if my child has special needs? How do I incorporate the arts into our homeschooling? The best advice I ever received as I navigated my own life journey was to find others who were doing what I wanted to do and ask them how they do it. *The Homeschooler's Guide to . . .* presents to you ten topics that you may have already found yourself wondering about and offers expert opinion on how to do it.

The beauty of this book is, it is written by people who know what your life is like—who like you are on a journey. Their expertise in a particular area is priceless! Not only do they know their area of expertise inside and out, they've also homeschooled and know the unique challenges that go along with it.

These ten topics are ones you might find at an area homeschool conference. But this book offers an in-depth discussion into each—something you can't get in a forty-five-minute workshop. If you have additional questions, you can ask the experts directly. Their contact information is provided for your convenience. Homeschoolers are generous people, willing to help one another along.

Keep in mind that there is more than one way to do anything, and this is especially true for homeschooling. You may not always agree with all of the advice presented here, but it gives you a starting point. So grab your favorite beverage and get comfortable. You're about to meet some very special friends!

1

TESTING AND EVALUATION

When I was a teacher in the public schools, my first exposure to homeschoolers was through testing. I volunteered to be a homeschool evaluator to make extra money. My previous experience as a teacher, but more specifically a special education teacher, offered insight into testing and evaluation that other teachers might not have. I knew there were many different kinds of tests used for many different reasons. I knew that individual assessment was just as valid as group assessment. What I wasn't prepared for was the homeschoolers' lack of understanding of the testing and evaluation process. For the most part, homeschoolers are quite intimidated by testing and the reflection it might have on their homeschools.

Later when I homeschooled our own two boys, I realized firsthand what the anxiety was all about. We had already accepted the responsibility to provide our children's education 100 percent, but at testing time doubts begin to fill our heads, and we question our abilities—even me, a teacher who knows a lot about testing.

Fear sometimes comes as a result of ignorance; so let's first get educated about testing. Then we can look at what to do after testing. It should be a constructive, not a destructive process.

WHY TEST OR EVALUATE?

For some this is not an applicable question. You may have no choice. Some states require year-end standardized testing each and every year. Other states offer several evaluation options. For instance, Florida offers five different options ranging from teacher evaluation to yearly standardized testing. Your first responsibility as a homeschooler is to know your state's regulations. You may not agree with those regulations, but you are still accountable to submit to them.

Many homeschoolers choose to test or evaluate their children, even if they are not compelled to do so by their state. There are some low-regulation states that do not require testing. Or your state may only require testing from the third grade on, and you want to start in first grade or kindergarten. Or maybe your state only requires testing every odd grade (i.e., third, fifth, seventh, etc.), but you want to test every year. There are various reasons why homeschoolers choose to test when they are not obligated to test.

• They want to establish a baseline to which they can refer year to year.

• They want to test every year just in case they put their child back into public or private school.

• They want an objective party to measure their child's success.

• Their umbrella school requires yearly testing even though the state does not.

• It is easier to test than to prepare for an evaluation.

• Their child has a weakness that they want to monitor year by year.

I'm sure there are other reasons people give for yearly testing, but these are the most commonly cited. There is not one right reason to test, just as there is not one right way to homeschool.

Each family's needs are different. Just be sure you are not choosing to test every year out of fear or peer pressure. Are you afraid you are not covering the material that you "should" and therefore want a test to hold you accountable? Are you testing every year because it seems like everyone you know is testing every year? Testing every year is only helpful if the test you use actually covers what you taught your child. For example, what if you choose to give the SAT (Stanford Achievement Test), which has a science and social studies component, but you know you did very little of either that year? What will those test scores tell you? Conversely, what if you did spend a lot of time on science and social studies but the version of the ITBS (Iowa Test of Basic Skills) that the district recommends doesn't test those areas?

Our state does not require yearly testing or evaluation. For my own children, we tested when the state said to and did teacher evaluation when they did not. We maintain "best work" portfolios, and it is quite easy to make an appointment with an evaluator and let him or her confer with my child about his portfolio.

Evaluations are less formal ways to assess how much and how well your child learned that year. If you had the choice between formal standardized testing and an informal evaluation, which would you choose? What are the advantages and disadvantages to each method?

ADVANTAGES AND DISADVANTAGES

• Standardized testing can offer validity, reliability, and objectivity, but is impersonal and can be stressful for some children.

• Informal evaluations offer personal one-on-one time with the student, but can be subjective.

• Standardized testing does not always offer parents enough detail in order for them to improve their teaching and their child's learning.

• Informal evaluations require preparation for both parent and child; some children may not be comfortable talking about what they learned with a stranger.

• Standardized testing requires test-taking preparation for those students who have never taken this kind of test.

• Standardized testing is frequently mismatched between curriculum and what is on the test.

If you have the opportunity to choose the evaluation option, your next step is to find an evaluator. Ideally, you should choose an evaluator who has experience with the standards of your child's grade level. If you choose a high school math teacher for your second grader, it may not be a good match unless that math teacher has experience with younger children and what they are expected to learn when. During mid-spring evaluators begin to advertise in homeschool support group newsletters. They may even post their name and contact information in a place that homeschoolers frequent. Whoever you call, make sure you ask for references from other homeschool families that this evaluator has worked with. Then follow up and call some of those families to see if they were satisfied with the experience.

Whether you choose to test or evaluate may or may not be within your control. If it is, choose the method that best suits your homeschool and your child's learning style. Sometimes it's not why we test, but what we test with that becomes an issue.

WHAT KIND OF TEST OR EVALUATION?

There are two distinct types of formal testing: *achievement* and *diagnostic*. A third, *aptitude*, is used primarily for students in eighth grade and higher to determine what areas of interest might lead to a career. For basic homeschool purposes, achievement and/or diagnostic are the most commonly used. There is one aspect to testing that you may not have considered before—your child's learning style. It plays a part in testing and evaluation as strongly as it does in learning.

Achievement

Academic achievement tests are usually given in groups with a proctor, cover the basic school subjects of reading, spelling, and arithmetic (although some tap into other content areas), and are computer-scored. The most commonly used academic achievement tests are the SAT (Standford Achievement Test), CAT (California Achievement Test), CTBS (Comprehensive Tests of Basic Skills), ITBS (Iowa Test of Basic Skills), and the SRA Achievement Series. Most recently individual states are devising state achievement tests. For example, Florida has the FCAT (Florida Comprehensive Achievement Test), and Colorado has the CSAP (Colorado Student Assessment Program). See the appendices for a listing of all states. Achievement tests are generally the required standardized tests for all students.

Diagnostic

There are also specific standardized diagnostic tests available. They are more systematic in their approach over a narrower range of content. They go more in depth to determine a student's strength or weakness in a specific content area. Reading and mathematics are the two most popular areas measured by a diagnostic test. One other difference between a diagnostic and achievement test is that some diagnostic tests are not timed tests. They are "power" tests by which one attempts to ascertain a student's maximum level of functioning. Generally, most diagnostic mathematics tests, for example, are power, rather than timed, tests. Some commonly used diagnostic tests are KeyMath Diagnostic Arithmetic Test, Stanford Diagnostic Mathematics Test, Stanford Diagnostic Reading Test, and the Woodcock Reading Mastery Test. Only a teacher, preferably one who is trained to instruct those with learning differences, is qualified to administer a diagnostic test such as these. Her interpretation of the results is crucial to discovering the next course of action regarding instruction.

A diagnostic test can be used in conjunction with an achievement test, especially if your child has a learning difficulty of some kind. These tests are not usually required by states and would be at an additional cost to you; but it is important to pinpoint your child's area of weakness if you are struggling to discover it yourself. Sometimes we know that he has trouble in math, but we can't put our finger on what concepts or skills our child is lacking. A diagnostic test can help.

Learning Styles Inventory

By this time you are most likely familiar with discussions about learning styles. In my book *The ABCs of Homeschooling* (Crossway Books, 2001),

I discuss matching your teaching style to your child's learning style. Take the concept one step further and take your child's learning style into account when you choose a testing or evaluation method. For example, if you have a child who is primarily a visual learner, he may become frustrated with a test that consists of listening to directions and filling in a computer-scored form. Or maybe you have a kinesthetic learner who can't sit still during the group-administered ITBS. Keep in mind that the traditional pencil/paper standardized tests elicit the best responses from strong auditory or visual learners.

If you haven't yet considered your child's learning style, you will find an overview of the different styles in the appendix of this book. In their book *A Parent's Guide to Standardized Tests in School* (New York: Learning Express, 1998), authors Peter W. Cookson and Joshua Halberstam address the issue of learning styles and testing. They offer test-taking strategies for each type of learner. I have adapted those strategies below for homeschoolers.

Test Strategies for Visual Learners

If you are administering the test yourself, be sure that your child reads the instructions himself or herself before answering a question. Even if you are required to read the instructions aloud, give him or her the opportunity to read them to himself or herself.

If there are charts or other visual information on the page, make sure he or she previews the information on those charts before attempting to answer any questions.

Test Strategies for Auditory Learners

Remember that auditory learners rely on the hearing of instructions. So if the test instructions say, "Read the instructions to yourself as I read them aloud," encourage your child to pay careful attention to your or the proctor's instructions. The less your child relies on his reading of the directions, the better.

If you have opted to test a young child (say, kindergarten through second grade), you might want to encourage him or her to read by moving his or her mouth, so that he or she actually hears what his or her eyes see. He or she may already do this naturally; allow him or her to do so.

Test Strategies for Kinesthetic Tactile Learners

Unfortunately, standardized tests are not at all kinesthetic-friendly. Sometimes these children fiddle with a ruler or pencil while doing work, but these things are not permitted during testing. As you prepare your child to take the test, help him or her develop his or her reading or listening skills.

If you are testing a young child, he or she may not be able to successfully adapt his or her auditory or visual skills. Allow him or her to hold on to some small object in his or her non-writing hand—perhaps a small ball or some Silly Putty. It will help him or her concentrate better.

If the test permits, provide scrap paper for your child. Be careful, however, that your child doesn't spend too much valuable time doodling instead.

WHO TO TEST OR EVALUATE

If you live in a low or moderately regulated state, you may have more choice as to who tests/evaluates your child than someone living in a highly regulated state. If you have such an option, consider this aspect of testing carefully.

Parent

Even though I am a certified teacher and very familiar with testing, it surprised me to find out that I could administer a standardized test to my third grader. When we lived in Florida, parents were not permitted to administer the tests, but here in Colorado we are—even though both states are classified as moderately regulated states for homeschooling. If you decide to administer a standardized test to your child, there are a few testing procedures I urge you to follow. These tests were created in controlled environments following specific protocols. All teachers who administer such tests must follow those same protocols to protect the reliability of the test. As a parent administering a standardized test, keep these protocols in mind:

• Use a timer for timed sections of the test—do *not* approximate.

• Read the directions aloud, and read them completely—repeat only where indicated.

• Read the section in the teacher's test booklet called "Administering the Test," and follow all outlined procedures.

• If your child tires easily, break up the sessions; do it in five days instead of three.

• If your child has never taken a standardized test, obtain a practice booklet to familiarize yourself and your child with the format and procedures. Never use the actual test as practice.

These protocols protect the integrity of the test and protect the integrity of you and your child. If you are not comfortable following these restraints, consider hiring a certified teacher to administer the test, or take your child to a testing center.

Certified Teacher

Certified teachers have had experience administering standardized tests at one time or another. They are quite familiar with the format and testing protocols. Since testing can take anywhere between two to eight hours, be prepared to compensate them for their time. Rates vary, so check locally as to the going rate. Many teachers willing to test or evaluate are registered either with your district's homeschool office (or liaison) or with area support groups. Some will even make presentations at support group meetings to let you know what their area of specialty is and what they charge for their services. If you have a relationship with a teacher in a public school, you could ask him or her if he or she is willing to test or evaluate your child. This is a good way for teachers to see what homeschooling is all about, especially when they do evaluations.

Another Parent

Some homeschool support groups or umbrella schools sponsor a testing week. You can send your child to a predetermined place to be tested. They will be proctored by other homeschool parents. Sometimes our children do better when they have to account to someone other than us. This is also good training for future testing situations, such as the SAT or the GRE (Graduate Record Examinations).

WHEN TO TEST OR EVALUATE

Again, for some of us there is no choice about when to test. Some states test twice a year, in the fall and then again in the spring. They use different forms of the same test. If you are doing the testing yourself and for your own purposes, choose a time of year that will indicate growth and learning in your child. It is recommended that you test at the same time every year in order to make valid comparisons of your child's progress. If you are not required by your state to test every year, you don't have to. Some parents choose to test every year regardless of what the state regulations say. The difference is that you only have to report the results every other year.

WHERE TO TEST OR EVALUATE

If you test your children yourself, you will obviously test them in your home. However, some circumstances may lead you to consider another testing environment. Maybe your child is too relaxed, and you are unable to get him or her to take the testing seriously. Or your child may be easily distracted, and the kitchen table just provides too many other things to look at. You may be unable to maintain a quiet, uninterrupted space for the administration of the test. For some children, even the dog walking by is too distracting. If these or other concerns have the potential to upset your testing situation, you might want to consider giving the test in a study room at your local library instead.

If you decide after all to administer the test in your home, keep these recommendations in mind: Provide a distraction-free area to administer the test. That includes a cleared table, an unplugged phone, no other children around, no television or radio on, and your complete attention as a parent.

You might decide instead to let your child take the test in a small group monitored by other homeschool parents. This is an ideal way to acclimate homeschooled students to the formal testing setting. Support groups and umbrella groups often host annual testing for a small fee. It is still important to prepare your child in the event that his inexperience with formal testing gets in the way of accurate results. He should be well rested, well fed, and wearing comfortable clothing for his surroundings. Even if the weather is warm, if the room is cold due to excessive air conditioning, he will be cold. Sometimes children will be allowed to have a bottle of water during the test. Check first with your proctors.

Districts often allow homeschoolers to take standardized tests in a school setting. If you are familiar with the school in which you are zoned, you can request that your child take the test with his school peers in a classroom. Again be sure to prepare your child for such a setting. If you choose this setting, you must let the district/school know well in advance. For April testing, let the school know at least by the beginning of January that you want your child to take the test there. They have to order the test form and answer sheet along with those for the other students. That will also give you a chance to practice test-taking strategies with your child from the practice booklets that the school also orders. Make sure you let the school know you would like the practice booklet when it arrives.

How to Interpret Results

Testing your child is just one hurdle for you as a homeschooling parent; interpreting the results of these tests is yet another. There are some measurement concepts that you should know before you open that envelope. Some testing agencies or districts include a pamphlet about how to read test scores, but others do not. Keep in mind that not all scores are created equal!

Percentiles

Percentiles indicate the percentage of scores that fall below a person's raw score. For example, if your child scores in the 94th percentile (94%) in spelling, that means that his score is better than 94 percent of all those tested when the test was created. The actual score itself is often called a *percentile rank*. Percentiles are the most commonly cited scores.

Grade or Age Equivalents

Grade or age equivalent scores try to compare your child's performance on the test to those of a particular age group or grade level. Age equivalents are expressed in years and months. For example, 6.6 means six years, six months old. Grade equivalents are expressed in years and tenths of years. For example, 7.2 means seventh grade, second month. Even though parents naturally gravitate toward comparing grade or age equivalent scores, these are in reality the least reliable types of scores. Do not rely on them.

Standard Scores

Standard scores are raw scores (the actual number of correct answers) that are transformed using a specified formula. You might see many types of standard scores on a test result form, including z scores, T scores, stanines, and scaled scores. Stanines are frequently used to report results. You can recognize a stanine as a 1, 2, 3, 4, 5, 6, 7, 8, or 9. 1s, 2s, and 3s are below average scores. 4s, 5s, and 6s are average scores. 7s, 8s, and 9s are above average scores. They provide insight into what achievement range your child is performing in.

The Bell Curve

Parents sometimes react negatively to a score that is lower than expected. For example, a 52 percent in reading comprehension seems like a failing grade, but not if you understand what a percentile rank denotes. That 52 percent means your child performed better on the reading comprehension part of the test than 52 percent of his peers who took that test when it was created. It helps to see how all the scores are related to one another. A 52 percent is an average score. All of these derived scores fall in and around the Bell Curve. If you understand the Bell Curve, it will help you keep all the scores that your child's testing reveals in perspective. The Bell Curve displays the normal distribution of many different types of scores including intelligence quotients (IQs). It isn't perfect, but it's what the schools use to interpret scores on standardized tests.

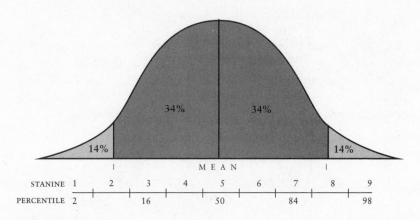

What Is the State Looking for?

Now that you have your child's test results in hand and can interpret them, you may wonder what will happen to them once you send them into your district or state office. Each registered homeschooling family has a file with the district. Your children's scores will be placed in that file. The district or state (depending upon who is the governing body over homeschoolers) is looking for "adequate progress." Adequate progress means measurable progress from year to year. If your child scored in the 60th percentile in mathematics in third grade and then the 62nd percentile in the fifth grade (with testing every other year), that is considered adequate progress. They expect the very same from public school children—adequate progress. So try not to panic if your child is in the fifth grade but his grade equivalent for language arts is 4.5. First of all, grade equivalents are not the scores districts look at. Secondly, you are looking for progress the next year. Some children may never perform at or above grade level in certain areas. The goal therefore is to progress.

YOUR OWN TESTS AND EVALUATIONS

Many parents wait until the end of the year to even find out how their children are doing. If the expectation is progress, the ideal is to pursue *continual progress*. Continual progress means to move from competence (or less than competence) toward quality in an area or skill. It is an active pursuit. Children experience continual progress in their daily lives. When they learned to walk, each day they were steadier and faster. When they learned to ride their bicycles, the more they rode, the less they fell and the faster they pedaled. Learning a concept or skill is the same.

When my youngest son, Charles, was learning his multiplication tables, he struggled. We did timed fact tests three times per week. His low scores on these tests initially frustrated him. He didn't like to be timed. However, if he didn't learn his multiplication tables, he would struggle in all math that followed. It is a foundational skill. Because he was having such trouble, I determined that he needed more practice time, and we actively spent time together memorizing facts. Slowly but surely he got better and better scores on his timed tests. His motivation increased because he now believed he could succeed. He made a goal for himself that he would get 100 percent of his facts on the timed test correct by the end of the month—and he did! That was definitely cause for celebration.

Testing can be used to drive instruction; that is, determine what your child needs to know, and then test again to see if he learned what he needed to know after instruction. It's a waste of time to teach or put your child through a curriculum that he has already mastered or conversely is so difficult that he cannot expect success. Below is a strategy for ensuring your child's success. It begins and ends with testing.

Pre-test

It is always advisable to pre-test your child on the material you plan to present, even if it is a unit study on Ancient Rome. This requires planning on your part. This requires that you actually know ahead of time what you are going to teach. If you use a published curriculum, there should be a pre-test or final test component. Give your child that test in the very beginning. You may be able to skip over much of the material and not waste time teaching things your child already knows. Pre-testing offers you a place to begin.

Teach

With your pre-testing results in hand, you can proceed with whatever instruction you had planned. Your starting point may not be at the beginning as originally planned.

Test

After you've covered the material, either give the test that accompanied your curriculum or devise a test of some kind of your own.

Reteach

Quite often your child's results may indicate that he did not gain a particular concept or skill after instruction. You have to decide if that is good enough, or if you want your child to completely understand the material presented. Reteaching is recommended if your child is missing crucial concepts or skills. You might have to teach in a different way or in a different format. When Charles still couldn't complete those multiplication facts, I had to investigate a new way to teach them to him. He is a very kinesthetic and visual learner; so instead of the drill fact sheets, we used a Learning Wrap Up® for multiplication. That way he could see the facts and use his hands to remember them better. He progressed quickly at that point.

Retest

Retesting is important to determine whether reteaching worked. Remember, if it is important to you that your child actually gains those concepts and skills and doesn't just push through the material, reteach and then retest. There is always the chance that retesting will indicate the need for more reteaching. It will show you what should come next—a new concept or skill or the reteaching of a previous one.

You will want to compare your child's performances over the years. You should use test results to make any instructional changes that might be necessary. There is a great debate over whether standardized test scores are appropriate for comparing children. No one teaches the same curriculum, even within states. No one teaches in the same way. Children are all from different social, ethnic, and economic backgrounds. There are so many variables. Your job as a homeschooling parent is to educate yourself about the process and implications of testing as they exist in your state. Then teach your children to the best of your ability and in line with how they learn. If you desire to provide your child with a quality education, you will do just that. No parent wants to be a bad teacher. Testing and evaluation have a language all their own. Learn the vocabulary. Understand the rules. Then be willing to be accountable for your homeschool.

RESOURCES

The Truth About Testing: An Educator's Call to Action by W. James Popham (ASCD, 2001).

A Parent's Guide to Standardized Tests in Schools by Peter W. Cookson, Jr. and Joshua Halberstam (Learning Express, 1998).

How to Do Your Best on Tests by Sara Dulaney Gilbert (Beach Tree, 1998).

2

HOME-BASED BUSINESSES

By Ellyn Davis
(THE ELIJAH COMPANY)

It seems lately that more and more homeschooling leaders are encouraging Christians to start home-based businesses. Because of these teachings, my family is continually approached by people intrigued with the fact that we operate a business out of our home or who want advice about starting a business of their own. In this chapter we would like to share briefly about how our business began, what it is like to have a home business, and some pros and cons of operating a business out of your home.

HOW THE ELIJAH COMPANY STARTED

The Elijah Company actually started because of the book *Alpha-Phonics*. Our oldest son, Seth, was a typical outdoors boy; so he didn't want to have anything to do with sitting down inside and learning things from a book. This wasn't really a problem, because we tend to have a flexible approach to learning; but we did want him to learn to read. We tried two or three reading programs that either bored him or that he thought were silly, and then I found *Alpha-Phonics* at our local library. In three months the child was reading. At that time (about fifteen years ago) it was practically impossible for homeschoolers to find good teaching materials. (Believe it or not, there was once a day when *no* educational supplier, not even Bob Jones and A Beka, would sell to homeschoolers!) So when I found *Alpha-Phonics* and saw what it did for Seth, I immediately called the publisher (who published all of Samuel Blumenthal's books) and asked if I could buy more for friends. He was a little puzzled by my request, and then a strange thought struck me. I asked him if I could have the distributorship for the homeschooling market. He said, "What homeschooling market?" and laughed.

By the end of the conversation, I was the sole distributor of Samuel

Blumenthal's books to the homeschooling market. I hung up the phone astonished at what I had just done and without a clue as to how to proceed. So from that humble beginning and after about fourteen years of homeschooling book fairs and catalogs, our business has grown from a few boxes of books in a corner of the bedroom to its own 2,000-square-feet facility. About five years into it, when the publisher realized that the homeschooling market was the biggest market for Blumenthal's books, he called me back and asked to be released from his commitment to me as sole distributor. By then we had added enough other products to our catalog that I was able to release him from the commitment. Now The Elijah Company employs five people full-time and takes on up to eight part-time workers on a seasonal basis.

THE HOBBY THAT ATE THE HOUSE

As you read my description of the growth of our business, you were probably impressed and thought, *Wow! Their business grew in twelve years from Mom and Dad and three kids boxing books and going to book fairs to its own building and up to thirteen employees!* Yes, it is impressive, and God has been very gracious to us to allow that kind of growth, but there's a hidden side to it all that anyone going into business for himself or herself needs to understand.

Home business means *home* business. For at least the first few years, everything about the business happens in your home. This means that paperwork is done on the kitchen table, whatever products you are selling are usually stored in some corner of your house, and you are essentially working two jobs, because it will be a while before any home business makes enough money to support the family. So unless you have lots of money set aside, you will have to keep working at your *real* job until the home business can become the real job. A home business is like having another child to take care of, and if you want it to grow, you have to feed it time, energy, and money.

The most interesting (and exhausting) aspect of a business is that there are benchmarks of growth, and each time the business reaches another level of growth (say, breaking the $50,000 a year barrier, then the $100,000 a year barrier, and so on), there will be a point at which you really need more help and more room but can't afford it. For example, for almost four years there were three to four employees working in my house every weekday—using my bathroom, getting things out of my refrigerator, sitting at my dining room table to eat lunch—you get the picture. It is only by the grace of God that I am a reasonably sane woman today.

So to all of you considering launching a business, we say, "Yes . . . but." Yes, having a home business is a wonderful blessing, but it's not as easy as it sounds. We have found that the lure of extra income through having a home business can be a subtle trap that undermines the very reasons we want to become more home-based. Along with its pros, there are many cons involved. At the risk of sounding negative, I would like to share typical problems encountered by those who run home businesses that you may never have considered. Think of what I share below as a home business reality check.

SEVEN COMMON MYTHS ABOUT HOME BUSINESSES

Myth #1: Having a home business means you will be able to spend more time with your family.

This is seldom true. In order for the business to reach the place where it can support your family (which usually takes five years or more), you will find yourself working much more than an eight-hour day. You will probably have even less time with your children than if you held down a regular job. Even though you are home in body, your attention will often be focused not on your family, but on your business; and there's no way to leave the office and go home, because the office *is* home.

Myth #2: Having a home business means you can pick your own hours to work.

Our friend Rob Shearer of Greenleaf Press laughs and says, "That's right. Having a home business means you can pick *which* sixteen hours of the day you want to work!" The reality is, no matter when you would like to work, you will eventually gravitate toward an 8-5 day because that is when your customers, employees, and services (banks, Post Office, UPS, etc.) expect you to be in operation. When the workday is done, there will still be things you have to do, and since the "office" is in your home, you will usually find yourself doing them. Also, because most home businesses are cash poor, you will have to do everything yourself for at least the first few years, which (even with spouse and kids helping) usually translates to much more than an eight-hour day.

Myth #3: Having a home business promotes family togetherness.

There are few businesses in which children can take an active part. Teenagers can be a great help if they have good spelling, reading, and math skills, but younger children are limited in their ability to contribute and are quick to resent the time, energy, and money toll the business takes on the family. It is complicated trying to devise jobs for each child and rewards for work that are commensurate with ability and age. Also, family businesses usually become "the hobby that took over the house." Few families can afford to build separate rooms for the business; so it overflows into the living areas. Tensions may mount because both Mom and Dad become overworked, the children feel neglected, the house is cramped and cluttered, and all available cash has to be channeled back into the business.

Myth #4: You can find your unique niche through a home business.

Yes, you can find a niche and may have little competition at first. But it won't be long before someone else will copy (or downright plagiarize) what you are doing, and they will probably offer your goods or services at a discount in order to get their own business off the ground. At this point you discover it's not as simple as finding a unique product or service—you have to offer more, cost less, do a better job, etc.

Myth #5: A home business can be a real ministry.

There is a tendency to view *business* as secular or worldly and *ministry* as spiritual. Early on you must decide that since you are a Christian, whatever you do for a living is also a ministry because *everything* a Christian does is ministry in one form or another. You are going to handle money Christianly, you are going to treat your customers Christianly, you are going to make business decisions Christianly, and so forth. However, your primary motivation is to provide for your family by *making money*. Because you are a Christian, you will naturally minister to others while you are making money. If you don't reach this conclusion, you will feel guilty for making money—especially if your business prospers.

Myth #6: The next best thing to a family business is for Mom to provide extra income at home.

Studies show that if a working woman with two preschoolers earns $40,000 a year, she is only left with about $4,500 after expenses. This means if she can net $4,500 per year at home, she has done as well as if she worked a $40,000 outside job. However, when a woman earns money at home, she brings into the home all of the stresses and clutter discussed in myths #1, #2, #3 and #4; and since her husband is not a part of this stress and clutter, tensions can develop. By far the most insidious consequences of a woman running a home business result from these two scenarios:

Scenario #1: Mom's business idea eventually is profitable enough for Dad to quit his job and come home. Because the God-ordained pattern of the husband being initiator and provider has been reversed, the husband and wife have to deal not only with spiritual issues of leadership within the home and business but also with gender issues because in many ways the husband and wife have exchanged roles and the husband's present success depended on his wife's business abilities.

Scenario #2: Mom's business idea grows to the point that she must find someone else (older daughters or hired help) to baby-sit the children and/or help run the household. In cases like this Mom might as well be holding down an outside job because she has withdrawn from the activities for which she stayed home in the first place.

We really want to emphasize this point because mom-run businesses are so common among homeschoolers. Listen to a homeschooling mother who found the pressures of running a successful home-oriented magazine overwhelming:

> Increasingly I was seeing the unfolding of a most disturbing phenomenon. . . . The longing for a home business was propelling homeschooling moms, sometimes with many small children, into establishing home businesses, hoping that they would be successful enough that their husbands could quit their jobs to come home. Sometimes the businesses did achieve moderate success and the husbands did come home. But because the woman had built the business, because it had prospered by way of her particular talents and gifting rather than the husband's, more often than not these women were finding themselves trapped: now they were not only keeping at home, often with heavy workloads and small children, they were also becoming the primary support of their families, the CEO, with their husbands and families dependent upon them, and not the other way around, even though the husband was often described as the overseer of the business. I have observed so many instances in which young mothers were literally at the breaking point, working from dawn until dusk, day after day, to get everything done, and often failing miserably. Any crisis—and in large families there are always crises—was a catastrophe, every interruption an emergency. The strain of attempting to combine so many roles is always debilitating and the guilt is tremendous, particularly during the years of bearing and nursing babies. With so much to do, nothing can be done well—not homemaking, not homeschooling, not being a good wife or mother. The inevitable result of this kind of overextension is exhaustion, poor health, loneliness, prayerlessness, and defeat.

Myth #7: You can start a business on a shoestring.

All businesses seem to operate according to the rule, *Whatever needs to be done will always cost much more than was expected.* You will need a fair amount of start-up capital to cover all the hidden expenses of going into business. Although this may sound exorbitant, you can easily spend a minimum of $25,000 of your own money getting a business off the ground. Then every time the business needs to expand you will need another influx of capital. (Think of it as a child that you have to keep feeding in order for him to grow.) This money has to come from somewhere, usually from your life's savings.

In addition to these myths, there are the depressingly true statistics that the majority of America's small businesses fail within five years.

Now that you understand the potential negatives of owning your own business, here is some advice on how you can make starting your own business a positive experience.

EIGHT HELPFUL HINTS ABOUT RUNNING A BUSINESS

Hint #1: Decide how much is enough.

Take a long, hard, realistic look at your family's needs, goals, dreams, and lifestyle. Determine how much it would take for you to live happily and peacefully within God's will. You may be amazed at how little you really need to live on and may find creative ways to come up with the needed money or to cut expenses to the point where you don't have to supplement Dad's income or engage in a business venture. There also may be ways Dad can make his present schedule more flexible and home-based. If Dad already has a good, steady job, remember that you will lose health insurance, retirement income, and many other benefits if he quits to go into business for himself.

Hint #2: Do a skills inventory.

Several organizations (such as Career Pathways) can help you determine the type of work best suited to your ambitions and abilities. You probably already are harboring a secret dream or desire that could be turned into a business opportunity. Take an earnest look at what you and your family members can realistically accomplish. In addition, you need to bear in mind that running your own business will require the following office and managerial skills:

• *The ability to manage time.* Not only will you have to meet deadlines and get to appointments on time, you will also have to plan ahead so that what needs to be done gets done when it needs to get done. You will need the inner resolve to stick to your priorities and not be swayed by "the tyranny of the urgent." Often your home business demands can usurp family time, personal time, friend time, and God time if you are not diligent about prioritizing your time.

• *The ability to handle stress.* This includes knowing your limits physically, emotionally, spiritually, and financially; knowing how to relax; keeping the big picture in view when the details are driving you crazy; developing satisfying hobbies; constructively dealing with anger and time pressure; etc.

• *An understanding of tax guidelines for home businesses.* Get IRS Publication #334: *Tax Guide for Small Businesses.* Search for a good accountant who can explain it all to you and help you get the most deductions possible.

• *The ability to handle money.* Owning your own business is always financially risky. Great care must be taken to use money wisely and according to scriptural principles. If money is your master, you will make rash decisions out of fear or greed. If you are already having trouble handling the family finances, get help before starting a business.

• *The ability to perform almost any office function.* No matter what your business, you will eventually be doing word processing, data management, spreadsheets, basic accounting, filing, etc.

• *The ability to get along with people.* There will always be someone who rubs you the wrong way, who tries to take advantage of you, or who misinterprets your words and actions. Good social skills and knowing how to deal constructively with conflict are essential. If you have employees, you will also have to develop good people management skills. If you directly interface with your customers, you will need to give special attention to your appearance, your speech and mannerisms, and social skills that make people feel appreciated.

• *The confidence to make decisions.* When you own your own business, that old adage "The buck stops here" applies to you. Hopefully most of your decisions will be right, but many will be wrong. You will have to be able to accept the consequences of your bad decisions and see failure as a valuable learning experience. Conversely, you will have to remain humble about your good decisions, because chances are you really didn't know what you were doing when you made them—God just covered for you.

Hint #3: Consider the ethical implications of your business ideas.

For the Christian, business decisions have spiritual implications. We cannot operate the way non-Christians do, even if it's "the American way." A capitalist, free-market economy works best for fallen man because it appeals to his desire to accumulate wealth and possessions—his desire for ownership and control of his life. The kingdom of God, however, operates under a different economic system, and there the desire for profit is tempered by the desire to bless others and a "brother's keeper" mentality. Business decisions that can have ethical consequences include:

• *Discounting.* If you undercut your Christian competitor's prices in order to increase your sales (by taking sales away from him), you rob your brother (or sister) in Christ of sales, you undermine his customer loyalty, you send the message to customers that price is the primary issue, and you send the message to your Christian brothers that sales is the only issue.

• *Exploiting relationships.* Some pyramid marketing companies tend to exploit relationships through having you build your sales success by getting friends and relatives to sign on.

• *Entering an already saturated market.* If there is a market saturated with vendors, you are jeopardizing the years of labor others have invested when you decide to sell the same products.

• *Building on someone else's idea.* Don't pick someone's brain about how they run their company and then become their competitor. Also, don't use someone else's idea unless you have their permission and give them credit and/or payment for it.

• *Using manipulative marketing techniques.* It is possible to create want with the right marketing techniques. Most advertising strategy is based on creating a desire for a product that people don't really need by appealing to the weaknesses of human nature. Manipulative marketing techniques persuade people to buy by appealing to their greed or pride or by causing them to fear what might happen if they don't buy the product. Other deceitful marketing strategies include overstating the merits or benefits of a product, creating pressure to make a quick decision by imposing deadlines, or giving the impression that the customer is getting a "bargain" by discounting an inflated price. Whatever goods or services you provide should meet genuine needs, and these goods or services should be marketed with integrity.

Hint #4: Study the market beforehand.

Check out whether the market is oversaturated with what you plan to offer, whether zoning laws will allow you to operate out of your home, what your competition will be like, etc., *before* launching your business idea. After it was too late we found out that the book business has the second lowest profit margin of any business (groceries is lowest). Also, every year more and more homeschooling families try their hand at selling books; so the market is supersaturated. (If you are considering selling homeschooling materials, *please* reconsider! Because the market is supersaturated with vendors, if you start selling homeschooling products, any sales you make will jeopardize the livelihood of families who have spent years servicing the homeschool market.)

Hint #5: Consider developing skills that are marketable anywhere and anytime.

The most lucrative and stable fields to enter are service industries like nursing, plumbing, electrical services, equipment repair, carpentry, etc. These skills are always in demand, even in economic recessions, and often allow flexible working hours. Our farrier (the guy who shoes our horses), who only works part-time, makes more than we do and has a marketable skill wherever he chooses to live. The man who did bulldozer work for us makes almost $100 an hour. Of course, he has the investment of his equipment, but this is nearly five times the salary that either my husband or I ever earned, and we both have Master's degrees. A homeschooling father in our small town does quality home remodeling and has a six-month waiting list. These may not be glamorous jobs, but they are lucrative, marketable, and allow for flexible schedules.

Another consideration is to pick skills you can pass on to your children. This way they can assist you while they are still at home, and they will have a trade when they are grown.

Hint #6: Learn how to handle money.

The apostle Paul said, "I know how to be abased, and I know how to abound" (Philippians 4:12, RSV). Christians seem unusually naive about money matters and are just as willing to go into debt as non-Christians. No matter how much or how little money you have, you must learn how to make it work for you. Find ways to cut expenses; to increase tax deductions; to stay out of debt; to set aside tithes, savings, and taxes. Most financial planning books are good, but not detailed enough. You will have to do a lot of reading and a lot of trial and error before you find a system that works for you.

Hint #7: Invest in people.

First invest in yourself, then in others. Whatever helps you or members of your family become more physically, emotionally, intellectually, financially, and spiritually productive is a wise investment. For years we drove a car so junky we had to climb through the windows to get in or out because the most productive use of our money was a good computer system.

Whenever we have extra money, we try and invest it in people: people's needs, people's ideas, people's talents, people's businesses. We're not talking about tithes or ministry, but about finding people we believe in and investing in them. If there is someone you trust who has an idea, vision, talent, or business needing financial backing, that is fertile ground for investment.

Hint #8: If there is a choice between more time or more money, pick more time.

Years from now, when your children are grown, you will regret the lack of time you spent with them rather than the additional thousands of dollars you could have made. Of course there will be seasons when finances become an important issue, but usually time is more important than money.

Consider this quote by Kermit Kuehn from the November 1994 *Quit You Like Men Magazine*:

Jesus said, "For what is a man profited, if he shall gain the whole world, and lose his own soul? or what shall a man give in exchange for his soul?" (Matt. 16:26). This question is powerful in itself, but when pondered in the context of "doing business," it becomes particularly pointed. Perhaps nowhere in life are we so in contact with, so engaged with the kosmos or world as in the case of making a living. . . . Business is the world's system, not the heavenly's. Its lures can so easily entrap us. It is only with a mind that is maintained in Christ that we are able to use this kosmos to further Christ's Kingdom on earth. What is our mind about business? Do we see ourselves as businessmen who happen to be Christians, or Christians who happen to be businessmen? The distinction is significant. We easily imagine the benefits of owning and operating our own business, but only too vaguely ponder its dangers. Our natural man seems to prosper in the soil of self-delusion, but our souls become easily impoverished.

ELEMENTS OF A SUCCESSFUL BUSINESS

In spite of the reality check presented in this chapter, I still want to encourage you to try your hand at starting a business. If you believe God is nudging you to start a home business, *do it*. One of the saddest surveys we ever read was taken at nursing homes. Elderly people were asked, "If you had the chance to live your life over, what would you do differently?" Their overwhelming answer was, "Take more risks."

Our home business gave our whole family opportunities and experiences we could never have had without it. It allowed the children to work alongside us and to travel with us throughout the United States; it taught us all valuable lessons in entrepreneurship, economics, self-management, and people skills; and it allowed us tax deductions for many of the things we wanted to do. It also gave us a deep appreciation for America and the freedom that we have in this country to pursue our dreams. But even more valuable than those experiences, having our own business made us reliant on God in ways we could never have imagined had Chris or I worked for someone else.

You can minimize the risks of starting and operating a home business if you know what to expect and do your homework beforehand. Becoming successful in any business is dependent upon four factors. Your strategy, no matter what type of business appeals to you, should be to:

• become educated as to what the market wants (this gives you your business idea);

• tailor your business to produce what the market wants (this gives you your business plan);

• make connections with people of influence in the industry (this gives you your marketing plan and support network); and

• become educated in how to operate a business (this gives you your business system).

All businesses start with an idea. There are hundreds of books and seminars on market trends, but the best place to start when searching for a business idea is to ask yourself two questions: (1) *What would I like to do?* and (2) *What need have I noticed that is not being met?* There is a good possibility that your hidden dreams and longings or the needs you are noticing are actually promptings from God.

An ideal way to examine your business ideas is to get about ten friends together to brainstorm. Share all of your ideas, and try to narrow them down to the one or two best ones. Have your friends add their suggestions and embellishments to your original ideas. When you come up with one or two ideas that seem to appeal to everyone, then develop the ideas on paper. A business should work on paper before it works in practice. Think through how the product will be marketed, how it will be packaged, what it would take to produce or develop it, and so forth.

The next step is to have everyone come up with objections—all of the problems that you might encounter or why the idea won't work. This is when you want your idea totally ripped apart, because your answers to these objections will define your business plan. If you cannot find satisfying answers to all of the objections, then the idea should be discarded or put on hold.

If your idea stands the test of the objections brainstorm and you have developed a business plan, it's time to study your market. Find out about advertising in your market, what the profit margin is in your market, who the opinion leaders are in your market, how successful businesses in your market are run, and so forth. Don't skimp on educating yourself, because it is so much easier to run a business when you have some sort of grasp of what you are doing than it is to learn as you go. (Trust me, I know from experience!)

In hindsight, I can tell you that the three biggest hurdles to ultimate success with a home business are (1) cash flow, (2) labor intensity, and (3) proper planning. If you think of a business as a body, cash flow is its circulatory system. Money flows in certain patterns, and you want to be sure that it flows correctly through your business so that the business thrives. Cash flow makes or breaks small businesses, because most businesses, even successful ones, have such small profit margins that there is hardly ever any extra cash available. If the concept of cash flow is new to you, you need to read *Cash Flow Quadrant* by Robert Kiyosaki.

In this body analogy, labor intensity is like the muscles of the body. Some businesses are much more labor-intensive than others; that is, some businesses require more labor to produce the product than others. When you are in your thirties, you may not mind lifting two and a half tons of books every week, but when you get to be fifty, not only are you tired of lifting them, but you really should not be doing it.

Continuing the body analogy, planning is the brain. This is why planning is so crucial. When starting a business, people seldom give thought to where they would like the business to be in five years, ten years, fifteen years, and so on, but this is exactly what they must do in order to increase the cash flow and decrease the labor intensity throughout the life of the business. Another very important part of planning is having an exit strategy. This is a technical term for: How would you get out if you ever wanted to? You probably assumed you would leave the business to your children, but what if they don't want it? You may have thought you could eventually sell the business, but if without you it loses its uniqueness, no one will buy it. So you need to plan for the life span of the business: how the business will begin, how it will grow, and how it will end.

TOP RESOURCES FOR HOME BUSINESSES

As the Preacher says in Ecclesiastes, "of making many books there is no end" (12:12, RSV), and that is certainly true when it comes to books about operating a business. We have read hundreds of business-oriented books, but there are less than ten that have had such an impact that I would recommend them to others. The first book I would recommend is Barbara Brabeck's *Homemade Money*. Called "the Bible of home business," this is the most comprehensive book available on the nuts and bolts of starting and operating a business from your home. Next, I recommend books by Robert Kiyosaki, particularly *Cash Flow Quadrant*. Kiyosaki's books tend to be repetitive, but they give an excellent overview of how money works in different types of businesses, and they stress the importance of owning your own business. His books will change the way you think about money and about business. The third series of books I recommend are by Robert Allen: *Multiple Streams of Income* and *Multiple Streams of Internet Income*. Allen's books are gold mines of ideas for different ways to create income. Finally, you need to read Richard Swenson's two books about how we tend to overextend ourselves physically, emotionally, financially, and spiritually: *Margin* and *The Overload Syndrome*. These books have nothing to do with home businesses, but everything to do with the underlying lifestyle that makes working at home a positive, satisfying experience.

COMMON QUESTIONS AND CONCERNS

Question #1: You are clear about the difficulties associated with running a home business, but can you talk about how certain personalities may thrive in such a situation?

Answer: To me, the key to thriving in the midst of all of that activity in your home has nothing to do with personality type. It has to do with vision. Deciding to take your kids out of public school and teach them at home required a change in paradigm about what education is, and staying sane with a home business requires a similar paradigm shift.

Think about it. What keeps you going in those tough times with homeschooling—those times when you begin to question why you ever thought homeschooling was a good idea? What keeps you going and grounded is a sense of vision and purpose—a sense that somehow in your feeble attempts to educate your children at home you are cooperating with God in the restoration of the family. You may not be doing everything perfectly, but you are at least claiming ground for the next generation. So all of your efforts, all of your victories and defeats, all of your joys and sorrows have a larger purpose than whether or not your children will get a better education at home or in the public school. Claiming ground is hard work. I'm sure the pioneers in the American West wondered whether they should have stayed back east where it was safer and easier and life was more settled. In a way homeschooling your children is a prophetic act, because it says to a generation who would rather abort their children than be inconvenienced by them that God has a standard, that parents have responsibilities, and that children are blessings from the Lord and should be treated as such.

Having a home business can also be a prophetic act. We live in a society trained to think of work as something we do as little of as possible, with others who look to a job (or to the government) to provide them with emotional fulfillment and financial security and who would rather have freedom restricted than take risks or face discomfort. Having your own business flies in the face of that way of thinking and becomes not only a means of providing for your family but also, by its very existence, a declaration of a vision.

Question #2: What can we tell the homeschool mom who worries that her home-based business has taken more precedence than she'd like over schooling?

Answer: In many respects, the ability to worry that our business may be taking too much time away from homeschooling our children comes from the privilege of being middle-class in a safe, prosperous democracy and from the mind-set that we are entitled to earn a decent living by putting in only forty hours of work a week. Millions of mothers do not have the option of expressing that worry. They are too consumed with putting food on their tables so their families can stay alive. Sometimes I think we forget to be grateful that we have the opportunity to homeschool our children and start our own businesses.

However, to those who *do* have the option of expressing that worry, I would say, "Close the business or find someone else to run it for you." That may sound like a flippant answer, but you have to ask yourself these questions: (1) Is running a home business *plus* homeschooling my children consistent with what God has told me to do at this season of my life? (2) Is having a home business (or the level of involvement I have in the business) strengthening my relationships with my family and my ability to properly nurture my children? (3) Do brothers and sisters in the Lord (particularly my husband and mature Christians in my life) wholeheartedly endorse what I am doing? If the answer to any of these questions is no, you should seriously examine whether you ought to be involved in a home business right now. You may have the right idea, but the wrong season of life. God does everything in times and seasons. In His economy, there is a time and a season for everything. But our tendency is to overlap—to combine what was meant for two seasons into one. If you have the luxury of being able to devote yourself to your children for a season, that is a priceless gift from God. Why would you devalue that gift and compromise relationships in order to have your own business? If you are not careful, your children will be grown and gone and you will regret the time the business took from them.

Question #3: How do families balance the needs of homeschooling and a business? Especially if they aren't "relaxed" or "unschoolers"?

Answer: Again, this question comes from a mentality of privilege and comfort, and of looking at a home business like it's going to suddenly make tens of thousands of dollars for you and be seamlessly integrated into your current lifestyle. You will be incredibly fortunate if your home business works that way for you. What is more likely is that your home business will turn your life upside-down.

Finding the balance between the needs of homeschooling and the needs of the business is tough, even when you are a "relaxed" homeschooler. Obviously, it is easier if Dad is the one primarily involved in the home business and Mom is the one primarily involved in the homeschooling. But part of the beauty of a home business is that it can become an entrepreneurial platform for the children, where they learn valuable business skills. If you are homeschooling using traditional methods, the children's involvement with the business may have to be minimal until they are in junior or senior high, and then you can build some business courses into your curriculum.

Ellyn Davis, mother of four, lives in Crossville, Tennessee, with her husband Chris and youngest son Blake. Her three boys have been home-schooled from birth, and she and her family operate three businesses: a homeschooling supply company called The Elijah Company, a publishing house called Double Portion Press, and a quarter horse breeding operation called Golden Opportunities Farm. Not only has Ellyn been active at home and with the businesses, but she also speaks at homeschooling conventions across the country. For more information about the Davis family and their philosophy of homeschooling, call 1-888-2-ELIJAH for a free catalog, or log onto The Elijah Company website at www.elijahco.com.

RESOURCES

Homemade Money: How to Select, Start, Manage, Market and Multiply the Profits of a Business at Home by Barbara Brabec (Betterway Publications, 1997).

Margin: Restoring Emotional, Physical, Financial, and Time Reserves to Overloaded Lives by Richard A. Swenson (NavPress, 1995).

Multiple Streams of Income by Robert G. Allen (John Wiley & Sons, 2002).

Cashflow Quadrant by Robert Kiyosaki (Warner Books, 2000). Also see his book *If You Want to Be Rich and Happy, Don't Go to School?* (Aslan Publishing, 1995).

3

COMMUNITY INVOLVEMENT

The big *s* word—*socialization*—rears its ugly head during every conversation about homeschooling in society at large. In a recent article published in a scholarly education journal, the author expressed fear that homeschooling "potentially dilutes active democratic citizenship" ("The Civic Perils of Homeschooling," *Educational Leadership,* April 2002). The debate has moved from whether homeschooled students are adequately socialized to whether they are good citizens. To be fair, many educational writers and experts are concerned about the new consumer mentality of parents. School choice opened this can of worms, so it's not just homeschoolers the author is worried about. My question to you is, can a homeschooler be a good citizen without being involved in his or her community? My answer is no. And since it is all about choice, we can choose to encourage our children to become involved with people and ideals outside their realm. The only way to do that is to actually step outside our comfort zone.

Volunteering is not natural for everyone. Some of us have to be forced to volunteer. I know that sounds like an oxymoron, but we know that some children don't comfortably take risks or try something new. They have to be nudged, sometimes even pushed into a new situation. That doesn't mean we leave them to flounder there in the new, unfamiliar environment, but we shouldn't enable them not to try either. Homeschoolers have to make more of a conscious effort to get involved in their communities, and many do a fabulous job. There are many ways families can volunteer together. There are also ways children can find their own niches and volunteer on their own. Volunteering should be viewed with the same courtesies and commitment as a job and treated with the same heart as a ministry. It is a way to work out in the world the values you are instilling in your children.

As a family we've made service in our church a priority. We have all found ways to use our gifts and talents to serve our church community. It wasn't until recently that we branched out into our Colorado Springs community. Our oldest son now attends middle school. He was accepted into the International Baccalaureate (IB) Program for advanced and highly motivated students. A requirement for this program is that each student must log volunteer hours within the community—half of those in service/people-related efforts and half environmental. Christopher chose to volunteer as a helper for the kindergarteners during Sunday school at church every other week. Even though only ten hours were required, he served in that capacity well beyond what was expected. He discovered that he enjoys working with young children. But serving within his home church was well within his comfort zone. In order to log his environmental hours, he needed to step outside of that zone and into the world.

Recently two opportunities arose to work as an environmental volunteer. Christopher spent a day planting new foliage at a nearby park. He didn't do it alone. His father and younger brother volunteered their time and energy there as well. Then he volunteered at the Hummingbird Festival here in town. Training was required ahead of time, and later he spent hours helping preschoolers and their parents make hummingbird feeders. I went with him for both the training and the volunteering. Christopher now feels comfortable engaging in activities outside his comfort zone. Because we walked him through it, he sees that it's safe and that he is capable of this kind of work.

We all need to look for ways to reach out to those in need. This doesn't mean you have to busy yourself to the point of detriment to your family, but it does mean modeling for your children what it means to volunteer. It's important to walk them through a new situation, especially if they are uncomfortable. That also shows them that you value their volunteer effort. If you volunteer as a family, that speaks volumes!

When I was growing up, my mother consistently encouraged me to volunteer. As a teenager she suggested that I be a candy striper in a hospital. When I was an adult, she thought I'd be good working in a hospice environment. My mother recognized that I had the gift of encouragement and pushed me to use it, but I didn't feel comfortable venturing out into those situations alone. My parents did not volunteer themselves. They believed it was important, but maybe it was too far outside of their comfort zone to do it themselves. Unfortunately, that influenced whether or not I would volunteer during those years. I rarely did.

I've come to learn that volunteer service is best accomplished when it uses your God-given gifts and talents. Then it isn't fearful. Then it isn't a chore. It is enjoyable! If you or your child are struggling to find where and how to volunteer in your community, first consider your spiritual gifts. Upon reflection you will then recognize what types of volunteering matches those gifts.

SPIRITUAL GIFTS AND VOLUNTEERING

Spiritual gifts are special abilities distributed by the Holy Spirit to every believer according to God's design and grace for the common good of the Body of Christ. These gifts should not be hoarded only to serve other believers. They can be used to build up the church (increase its numbers) or to equip the saints. Identifying your spiritual gifts will help you plug in more effectively. Spiritual gifts are different than talents. Talents such as musical ability, artistic skills, and athletic skills are also gifts from God, but they are given to benefit mankind in its natural life. "Spiritual gifts, on the other hand, are given for benefit in the realm of the spirit, the realm of an individual's relationship to God. The effect of the operation of a spiritual gift is to improve a person in his spirit's enjoyment of the life and love of God—to bless him, in other words" (*Body Life* by Ray Stedman, Regal Books, 1972). Exercising your spiritual gift(s) is always a satisfying and enjoyable experience, even if the circumstances within which you serve are not.

Below you will find a brief description of commonly recognized spiritual gifts. Search the Scriptures about spiritual gifts on your own. This list is adapted from a paper presented in a series called "Now Concerning Spiritual Gifts. . ." by Ron R. Ritchie.

• *Prophet*: The spiritual ability to speak forth the mind and counsel of God. Prophets in the church equip the saints for ministry within the church (Ephesians 4:11-12) and also edify, comfort, and encourage believers and reveal the secrets of men's hearts (1 Corinthians 14:23-25).

• *Evangelist*: The spiritual ability to communicate the good news of Jesus Christ's redemptive story to a dying world lost in sin and shame (Romans 3:23; Ephesians 4:11).

• *Pastor-teacher*: The spiritual ability to shepherd the flock of God (guard, guide, encourage, warn, etc.). Pastor-teachers continue to be placed in the Body of Christ to feed the Word of God to the flock of God, as well as to equip believers to find their spiritual gifts so they can do the work of ministry (Ephesians 4:11-12).

• *Serving*: The spiritual ability to meet the physical needs of men and women within the Body of Christ and those living within the surrounding communities (Acts 6:1-6).

• *Teaching*: The spiritual ability to explain truth from the Word of

God clearly so that the disciples of Jesus can understand it and apply those spiritual truths effectively in their daily lives (Acts 18:24-28).

• *Encouragement*: The spiritual ability to come alongside persons who may be hurting spiritually or emotionally and offer them a word of comfort concerning the past and a word of encouragement, admonishment (truth in love), and challenge so they will be able to walk in the steps of the Spirit in the future (Acts 4:36-37).

• *Giving*: The spiritual ability to give financially or materially to the needs of others within the Body of Christ or the community in which believers live. They express this spiritual gift with liberality and in simplicity to the glory of God without drawing attention to themselves (Acts 4:36-37).

• *Leadership*: The spiritual ability to provide guidance, direction, vision, and clarity for other members of the Body of Christ as they seek to participate in various ministries (1 Timothy 3).

• *Mercy*: The spiritual ability to manifest pity and give aid to those who are physically, emotionally, or spiritually helpless; the spiritual ability to express compassion and lift up the downtrodden with cheerfulness (Acts 9:36ff.).

• *A word of wisdom*: The spiritual ability to perceive life and truth from God's perspective and then apply that wisdom to specific situations within the church or the world (James 3:17).

• *A word of knowledge*: The spiritual ability to communicate spiritual truth to fellow believers that has been acquired through the investigation of God's Word, so they may grow into spiritual maturity (Acts 18:24-28).

• *Faith*: The spiritual ability to see what isn't, believe it to be, and trust God to do it in His way and time (Acts 3:1-10; 6:5).

• *Discerning of spirits*: The spiritual ability, on the basis of God's Word, to discern between the spirit of evil and of God, between the flesh and the spirit, and between truth and error before the fruit is evident (1 John 4:1-3).

• *Helps*: The spiritual ability to come alongside others and support them and their ministry in physical ways (see Paul's list of friends in Romans 16:1-15).

• *Administration*: The spiritual ability to give guidance, to pilot, to steer. The spiritual ability to be a helmsman for a local church in helping direct its life, order, and vision. One who deals with people and not paper (1 Corinthians 12:28).

Spiritual gifts, used in conjunction with talents God has given you, will help you serve in your church and in your community with joy and thanksgiving! A spiritual gifts inventory is included in Appendix III for your use. Keep in mind, however, that different writers may develop different inventories. This is just one.

Top Places to Volunteer

Finding a place to use our gifts and talents is sometimes trickier than discovering those gifts in the first place. When your children are young, try to expose them to many different ways to volunteer. Their own spiritual gifts may not be revealed until they are at least twelve or older and will continue to develop. Remember that their spiritual gifts may not be the same as yours; so as they mature, don't insist that you always volunteer together as a family. What you choose may not match with their gifts, and if you try to force the situation, it will be a miserable experience for all of you. Every conceivable organization or foundation in your community has ways for you to volunteer. Many have websites with links for this very purpose. Check the bulletin boards at your church, in your child's school (if applicable), and where you go for recreation. A great place to check for ideas on the web is www.networkforgood.org. That site also offers you a way to log your volunteer hours if that is important to you in your homeschool. Below are categories of volunteering to get you started:

Animals and environment. Thousands of charities are working to protect animals and the environment so that future generations will inherit clean air and water as well as an abundance of plant and animal life. Examples of organizations that focus on these issues are The Audubon Society, your local parks and recreation departments, wildlife conservation and preservation organizations, local zoos or animal or bird sanctuaries, national forest and trails maintenance organizations, and pollution cleanup and prevention and energy use organizations.

Arts and culture. Nonprofit organizations that support the arts and culture help to preserve the past, share the present, and imagine the future. These organizations need your help, whether your support is in the form of a donation, your time as a volunteer, or speaking out on the causes that matter most. Examples include museums, the National Endowment for the Arts, and organizations working with indoor or outdoor art, music or drama outreach, media, and journalistic endeavors. Local areas sponsor festivals throughout the year to raise awareness of the arts and culture, and they always need volunteers.

Civic and community. Many nonprofit organizations focus on improving our communities and protecting our civil liberties. These organizations will benefit greatly from your donations, time, and support to help protect individual rights and sustain efforts to better our communities. Organizations that support the efforts and ideals of people in your community who need help include groups that benefit children, ethnic communities, fire fighters, police officers, other rescue workers such as the Red Cross or the Salvation Army, Neighborhood Watch, your local schools, etc.

Education and research. Education is an important foundation for personal success and growth. Many nonprofit organizations are working to ensure access to education programs, especially for disadvantaged youth, immigrants, seniors, and people with disabilities. You could sponsor an international student, work to improve literacy in youth and adults, be a mentor or work in dropout prevention, tutor a student for free, etc.

Health. With so many illnesses that can devastate mind and body, the demand for medical research, information, and treatment options is never-ending. Every major disease is represented by nonprofit organizations working to support research, public awareness, and education, as well as public policy. You can participate in a walk to raise money, volunteer at a health fair, visit sick children and their parents, etc.

Human services. Thousands of charities provide support and services to our citizens—young, old, poor, and disabled alike. These services cover everything from food and housing to disaster preparedness and legal services. You can help with job placement, homeless families, food pantries, foster parenting, etc.

International. Around the world, nonprofit organizations work to ensure basic human rights and to provide education, medical care, disaster relief, and other services. You could work or support relief efforts overseas, work to build bridges between cultures, even become a pen pal!

Religion. We live in a world with many religions: Christian, Jewish, Muslim, Buddhist, Hindu, pagan, and everything in between. Most of the major religions, along with other nonprofit organizations, offer a variety of faith-based services, including soup kitchens, job training programs, and homeless shelters. You may be more comfortable serving in your own church community in some way. Outreach in conjunction with your church is also a good way to volunteer.

THE CHARACTER TRAITS OF A VOLUNTEER

Every organization can list what in its view makes a great volunteer, but some basic character qualities are valued by all those we serve.

An effective decision-maker. Volunteering is a choice. It should not be forced participation. Was this decision made with great consideration, counting the cost? Organizations don't want someone who flits from place to place. They are looking for someone with a sense of commitment.

An independent worker. Once you are given instructions, can your supervisor walk away confident that the job will get done? If you have questions, do you seek out the answers or sit idle and confused? It does an organization no good if supervisors have to spoon-feed the volunteers. Be someone who takes initiative, who completes the job without being reminded to do so.

An effective communicator. Volunteers are counted on as if they are paid employees, although oftentimes they don't act in that way. If you will be unable to complete a part of your assignment, give the organization notice well in advance so they can find a replacement. Make sure you have the contact information for whoever is in charge, and keep it in a safe place. Make sure any and all contact you have with your supervisor is pleasant, showing a willingness to do whatever he or she needs you to do. Your tone of voice should always be respectful.

A quality work producer. You won't be much help if someone else has to redo a job you were supposed to do. Make sure your work is done correctly and completely. If you don't understand how to do something, ask. A job worth doing is a job worth doing well!

A creative problem-solver. There are times when things don't go as planned or you run into a situation for which your supervisor did not prepare you. What will you do? Some people just pretend the situation or problem doesn't exist and ignore it. Look for ways on your own to solve the problem instead. If you still have difficulty, find someone who knows what to do and ask.

An effective leader. Jesus was the ultimate leader—He was the servant-King! Even if you are put in charge of something, fulfill your duties with a sense of service. Serve those put under you. They will then be much more willing to follow.

A cooperative worker. Many service opportunities are carried out in groups. Do you get along with others? Are you willing to take a subservient role? If personalities clash, can you be a peacemaker? If the group doesn't work well together, the work doesn't get done.

A time manager. Time is a precious commodity, especially for volunteers. Often you are volunteering after your normal school or work hours, and it is time taken away from your family. Treat that time and the time of others with respect. Be on time. Finish on time. Redeem the time whenever you can.

Our children don't possess all of these qualities at this moment; in many cases neither do we. Volunteering not only helps others—it helps you develop these traits yourself. And these traits will serve your children well when they get their first jobs, when they leave home, and when they raise families of their own.

CALLED TO COMMUNITY

As homeschoolers it's easy to become isolated. Teaching our children takes a great deal of time, energy, and commitment. Sometimes it's hard to look outside the window and say, "Where else can I serve You, Lord?" This is not to say that teaching your children shouldn't be your priority. But be careful not to let that become an idol. We need solitude in order to contemplate our current state and what work God expects us to do. We need community in order to be supported and nourished in preparation for that work. We need ministry to live out that work. Ministry is for the church as well as for those outside the church.

We are not called to be alone. For what purpose then would these gifts and talents exist? "As each has received a gift, minister it to one another" (1 Peter 4:10, NKJV).

If we seek community with family, friends, churches, prayer groups, etc., we will experience love, acceptance, forgiveness, and celebration. Often we seek community after we've first experienced solitude. Within community we are equipped for ministry. If you are not in community with other Christians and find yourself still in solitude, take the risk and grab another solitary soul and create community together. If you do not have a home base from which to work or volunteer, you will run out of steam and most likely quit. We all need the protection, equipping, and sustenance of a community. Make sure this house is in order before you venture outside.

In the United States, citizenship is linked with the volunteer spirit. We are an independent people; yet we couldn't survive if it were not for the kindness of strangers. So many of us gave blood in the wake of September 11, but our local blood banks are in desperate need. Some of us sponsor a child in another country for food, medical supplies, and an education, but the fastest-growing homeless population is that of children here in the U.S. A survey of twenty-five U.S. cities found that in 2000, families with children accounted for 36 percent of the homeless population (U.S. Conference of Mayors, 2000). Single mothers and children make up the largest group of homeless in rural areas (Yvonne Vissing, *Out of Sight, Out of Mind: Homeless Children and Families in Small-town America*, The University Press of Kentucky, 1996). We don't have to look past our own backyards to find people in need. It may even be your neighbor who is alone at every holiday, or your child's soccer coach whose wife just left him. If you want to use your gifts and talents for others, you won't have to look far.

Homeschoolers are greatly advantaged when it comes to volunteering in their communities. First, we have a heart for ministry that extends beyond our own families. Second, we have time because our school days are flexible. Certain writers are concerned that consumerism in education is a danger to civic responsibility, but it's not homeschoolers who are to blame. The more visible we are in our communities, the more our communities will see us for who we really are. What better advertisement for homeschooling could there be? This is more powerful than test scores or winning the National Spelling Bee!

RESOURCES
Body Life by Ray Stedman (Regal Books, 1972)

4

HIGH SCHOOL AND COLLEGE ENTRANCE

By Shari Henry

The summer before my son entered eighth grade, his circles of friends and activities he was interested in both grew wider than I'd ever expected from my relatively reserved child. By the next spring he was talking about wanting to attend high school. He wanted to go to school with his friends.

Up to this point he had made very good decisions based on sound reasoning. So his father and I saw our job to be listeners more than anything. We watched our son think, plan, compare, and begin a more structured curriculum to help him prepare. I researched the entrance requirements of the local schools, talked to teachers and counselors, and marked the registration date on the calendar. We talked about the pros and cons of school attendance, and those of staying home. Though we walked beside him and brought a large dose of maturity and wisdom to the process, his father and I trusted his ability to make a decision that was right for him.

Only a few days before registration, my son said to me, "You know, I really don't have peace about going to school." And so it was. For us. But other homeschoolers make other decisions based on their children, their families, and what seems best in their circumstances.

Now we are helping the same son prepare to take his college entrance exams. The weight of some of the decisions we are making does not escape me. I can't promise you that you won't sometimes feel a heavy burden for your children or that anxiety won't wash over you as you face these same sorts of decisions. I can tell you that if you approach decisions regarding high school and college with the same conscientiousness that you approached raising children and homeschooling in the first place, you will know where your peace comes from and will rely on God. Start researching early, and spend ample time on your knees. Then move forward in confidence that you know your children best of all and can help them tap into all the great resources they've learned (academically, emotionally, spiritually) in their years of homeschooling. Don't forget—rarely is any decision irreversible. Reserve the right to change your mind.

WHERE ARE YOU GOING?

While it's unrealistic to expect most young teenagers to have their life's goals mapped out, the years prior to high school are a good time to take stock of your homeschool. Ask questions. Where have you been? Have you accomplished those things you had hoped to by now? Why or why not? Where are you now? Do you see the character traits you had hoped for in your teenage child? Has he or she mastered the basic skills? Is your student academically and emotionally ready for a rigorous high school course load? Have any developmental or other learning problems been remediated to the best possible solution? If not, take action. The high school years are filled with enough hard work without continuing to struggle with an ongoing learning problem. Seek correction for the problem or reasonable good coping skills. Finally, where are you going? Is your child college-bound or do you need to help your student find course work and internships that will allow him or her to move directly into a meaningful career? Either way, be sure whatever schooling option you choose is a realistic preparation for getting your student ready for the future.

Time does seem to fly by. Our children grow as tall or taller than we are, learn things we may not have ever learned, and form relationships with more people outside of our family. A number of homeschooling children decide to attend high school with their parents' blessings. Many others stay home for their high school years. There are many great reasons for choosing either. Online educational opportunities are increasing constantly, creating even more options for students. Look for an educational environment that will equip *your* student. Regardless of where your child attends high school, remember that your family has the primary responsibility for education.

SO YOU WANT TO GO TO HIGH SCHOOL?

I've had many good homeschooling friends whose children attend high school in a traditional setting. A local private high school actively recruits homeschoolers. Another local private high school's administration is brainstorming ways to offer certain classes to homeschoolers. Private schools often make a good choice for homeschooling families since the parents in these schools are allowed more input and freedom of choice than in most public school environments. Also, these schools tend to be smaller with more accessible teachers than in the public schools.

At the same time, most private schools do not offer nearly the amount of extracurricular activities that students enjoy at the average public school. While private schools have some athletic teams and clubs, for example, sheer numbers dictate that the public school will have a far greater number. Also, private schools are often costly, whereas public education is free. Public schools often boast good drama and music departments, reputable bands, and a wide variety of sports teams and academic clubs as well.

Only you can answer whether your child would be better off at a private or public school, but do take a look at all of your options; be bold about interviewing teachers or counselors, asking questions of other parents, and so on. Familiarize yourself with available options within your school laws. Though the situation is improving, often school administrations do not know as much about transitioning your child from home to school as you do. A friend recently dropped by a school's guidance office to pick up the proper forms to enroll her son as a ninth grader in the public school. This child was far ahead of his peers both in maturity and academics. However, the counselor asked, "What makes you think we will have a place for him?" The mother calmly but firmly answered, "Because, sir, it is the law." Public schools *must* find room for your child.

Readiness

If your child has worked through a fairly traditional eighth-grade curriculum, there is no reason to think he will not be academically ready to attend the ninth grade. Most homeschooling curriculums are at least equal to, and are often more advanced than, most of those offered in public schools. If your approach has been more eclectic or relaxed, or if you have been unschooling, you may want to ask the school if you can borrow some of the ninth-grade texts to see if they look like something your child could reasonably handle. All homeschoolers I have known who have chosen more eclectic methods of homeschooling have been fine, though some have found gaps here and there (just as they also find areas where their children have a broader range of knowledge than their schooled peers have). If your child has a particular weakness or learning disability, ask the school how it handles such things. Schools deal with such students all the time. However, you may not want to share too much. Your child should be able to attend school without a host of labels. Use discretion.

Some schools may ask for transcripts. Depending upon how you have approached homeschooling, you may or may not have them available. If you belong to a covering school or have used a large curriculum company with academic services, you should have transcripts that look like the school's. Don't be shy about writing your own. Or outline the body of work your child has completed in a notebook, scrapbook, or portfolio (this is good for college admissions also, if you choose homeschooling for high school).

The vast majority of schools want to see standardized test scores. You need to plan for these the February or March prior to school entry (school registration and orientation dates are usually in March and April). Check with your covering school or local support group for help if your child has not taken standardized tests. Christian Liberty Academy offers testing services for homeschooling families. For a small fee they provide the testing materials and will score the test for you (847-259-4444, ext. 6, www.homeschools.org).

Schools also require complete health forms. Plan ahead for a thorough doctor's exam based upon school requirements. Ask for the school's form ahead of time, and take it with you to the doctor's office.

You may want to schedule a meeting in late winter or early spring to be sure you are on track in pulling together anything else the school administration requires.

What Schools Expect of Students

Educators expect that students will get along well with others, are able to find their way around, and realize they are part of a group and not merely individuals most of the time. On average, high school teachers deal with twenty-five to thirty students for five different class periods a day. While most would say they are interested in individuals, it's not realistic to think they can accommodate students' every mood, desire, learning style, and need or area of interest. Students need to follow set rules for the safety and management of the whole. This may be hard for children who have been homeschooled all of their lives. While parents can schedule conferences and can phone teachers, teachers have full personal lives and may not always be available when parents want them to be. You won't have nearly the input or control that you had all those years with your child at home.

High school students are expected to handle the majority of their own problems. Students are expected to listen and learn, keep up with schoolwork, and let the teacher know if they have questions. Students take notes in a lot of classes, which might initially be a challenge. If you know ahead of time that your child will be attending school, encourage him or her to take a class through a co-op or covering school, or practice by taking notes during church sermons. Note-taking is not hard, but it takes practice.

Students are expected to meet deadlines. Hopefully in the years you've homeschooled, your child has learned to take responsibility for his own work. However, few homeschool parents enforce strict deadlines. We don't have to, and we tend to want our children to work more toward mastery than meeting a deadline. Schoolteachers do not have the liberty of operating the same way, nor would it be practical for them to do so. This may take some getting used to; so be prepared to help your child figure out a system whereby he or she can schedule his or her time better in order to meet deadlines. It would be a shame to have excellent work graded down because of being turned in late.

Students are expected to show up. Make no mistake about it—school laws are much more geared toward attendance than they are toward education (this is not to say teachers and educators feel this way, but the laws are written this way). Students draw unwanted attention if they are absent too much. Most likely, high schoolers will not be able to stay up as late, read in bed until the wee hours of the morning, or do some of the other things they may have become accustomed to doing while homeschooling. The school bell rings early for most kids used to homeschooling. They'll get used to it, but they need to be there, and on time.

What Students Can Expect from School

Your child can expect a lot of friendships to have been formed among the kids who have been attending school together for years. They need to know it may take a while to find a way to fit in. Your student can, however, decide to look for opportunities to do so. There are clubs, organizations, sports teams, and other groups to which your child will make a great addition. Balancing the need for finding a group to enjoy with taking the time necessary to make sure they are people with whom it's worth spending time is well worth the effort. All students feel overwhelmed and very tired at times. So will yours. In time, though, they will feel a sense of accomplishment in what they're doing, a sense of belonging to a community of people with similar interests (band, football, math team, etc.). Rising to meet challenges will pay off in strong relationships and self-confidence. Finally, students should expect, even demand, that the school get them ready to pursue their future goals.

As parents you need to continue to be available for your children, help them when they need it, listen, direct, and guide. At first you may feel a distance forming; so plan on scheduling time to be sure you aren't losing your children to their peers. Stay in touch. Talk, pray together, worship together, go out to lunch, shop, enjoy one another. Also, be sure your schooled children find ways to spend time with their homeschooled siblings. Too many siblings separate emotionally when one child begins attending school. The schooled child will be away from home a lot, but with some forethought and planning, siblings can (and must) find things to do together.

Parents: Tell the Truth

All the homeschooling parents I know attended school when they were growing up (though I'm sure a handful out there have some great stories about being homeschooled well before it was popular to do so). We all know what school was like and can be assured it hasn't changed for anything but the worse since. At the same time, schools have a lot to offer our children or we wouldn't allow them to attend. Please don't feel like you have to sugarcoat the truth in order to protect your child. They'll see it or hear it soon enough upon entering the building, rest assured.

When my son was thinking of going to school, we told him we'd support his decision no matter what. We meant it. However, I wanted him to know it was going to involve more than spending time with his friends, playing sports, and attending class. I reminded him of the early hours he'd have to rise, how he might have to limit some of his sports activities accordingly, etc. When we drove by the school, I would be honest about how frustrating it is at times to be a teenager cooped up in an institutional building all day every day. That local school is falling apart (plans are underway to build a new one). Aesthetically, I believe it robs something from our children to be in an institutional setting so much, and I would point this out to my son. No more getting up without an alarm. No more hot chocolate mid-morning while working out math problems on the living room couch. No more reading great literature in bed or taking a spontaneous extra few days on an out-of-town hockey trip in order to visit grandparents, aunts, uncles, and newborn baby cousins.

I didn't tell my son these things to discourage him. I wanted him to be braced for the reality and make a wise choice based on all the facts. I told him that as much as he liked his friends, he might not like them as much when he was with them five days a week, seven hours a day. Then again, he would most likely make more friends and be able to be in on what was happening at any given time instead of counting on someone remembering their homeschooled pal and calling him to include him in moviegoing or bowling.

Support Your Child

Once you, your husband, and your child have spent ample time evaluating your options, praying, and preparing for school attendance, don't look back.

Support your child, and support the school. Become active where appropriate, and encourage your child to do the same. Go for the whole experience of the good that the high school years have to offer. When your child gets discouraged, don't say, "This is why we probably should have made you stay home." Do not undermine your child's confidence in his or her abilities to figure things out and work things through. Help your student succeed.

Of course, only you can know when and if things get so bad that the kind of support your child needs is the permission to quit and come home. Just know that hundreds of homeschooling children have made successful transitions into traditional school life and are often the best and brightest and most involved students at those schools. Make it your first priority to help your child be one of those.

Note to Students: Equip Yourself; Stand Your Ground

Parents would do well to pass on to their child the following thoughts: Student, do all you can do to get yourself ready academically, emotionally, physically, and spiritually. Be prepared to make some hard decisions, but know you can make them. Find a group of like-minded students. Join a prayer group or Bible club. Don't leave yourself as a lone ranger trying to stand against the tide of mass peer pressure without a life jacket.

HIGH SCHOOL AT HOME

Now back to the parents. If you have been homeschooling awhile by now, you most probably have given homeschooling during the high school years a lot of thought. If you are still three or four years away from the high school years, now is the time to start planning. If high school has crept up on you, or if your child is attending high school now and you need to bring him home, it's not too late. The homeschooling community is full of people who have forged the high school path for you; so by all means, get busy and ask questions. You'll find your own way, but they can help.

Now is the time to evaluate the strengths and weaknesses of your homeschool and to set goals for the high school years. It's time to gather facts about what constitutes a core of studies for most high school degrees, whether or not you need to take the GED (General Educational Development test; 800-626-9433; www.gedtest.org), how to prepare for college entrance exams, what your local truancy and work laws are (call your child labor office or ask other homeschoolers), look for apprentice opportunities, and research what various colleges look for in applicants. This is a time to shore up weaknesses too. Let your high schooler help. Generally children assess themselves pretty honestly; and if your child doesn't, it's a good time to help him or her learn to do so.

Evaluate Options

More options than ever are now available for homeschooling high school-ers. I've listed the most common.

Going It Alone

Many homeschooling families continue to go it alone during the high school years, the parents and students taking full responsibility for over-seeing the student's education. Curriculum companies have greatly improved their offerings. If you haven't already, get plugged into a local and/or state support group, attend curriculum fairs with your student, and choose materials that will work best for you. Cathy Duffy's book *The Christian Home Educators' Curriculum Manual: Junior/Senior High* (Grove, 2000) is full of curriculum reviews, planning ideas, courses of study, testing, and college application information. Familiarize yourself with the various companies and what may work best in your home for your needs, then start ordering.

Co-ops and Trades

I know few homeschoolers who completely go it alone during high school. At the very least, most families (like ours) trade a subject or two. For exam-ple, a friend teaches my son his lab sciences, and I have helped her daugh-ter with writing. Our students get the benefit of working with another student on lab assignments, and I am off the hook for a subject I am not so comfortable teaching! If your child is weak in an area that you also are weak in, start asking around and see if you can work a trade.

Co-ops are growing in popularity all of the time. They work much like trades, but on a larger, more structured scale. Students pay for and attend a certain number of classes, and parents teach another subject as part of the co-op deal. Ask around in your state group to see if any co-ops are already operating. If not, don't be afraid to try to start one.

Covering/Umbrella Schools

Many curriculum providers also offer teaching and advisory services. When you're evaluating curriculum, consider this option. It may help your child learn to meet deadlines, while also taking pressure off of you.

There are national umbrella schools and curriculum services that will, for a fee, provide advisors to families to help evaluate options, keep track of work, and provide transcripts. Again, ask your support group for a list, look for ads in national homeschooling magazines, or search online.

Some states have covering school laws; others have covering schools available even without a law prescribing such. These schools range from very little oversight and accountability to those with actual buildings where children meet for classes, attend proms, purchase yearbooks, and receive high school diplomas. Asking nearby homeschoolers for recommendations is the best way to find a covering school near you.

Online Education

Some curriculum companies provide online advisors, and others are exclusively online—students submit work over the Internet and receive graded work back from a teacher. These online academies offer diplomas, keep track of transcripts and course work, and often help with the college application process. Three examples of this are: Bridgestar Online Academy (www.switched-onlineschoolhouse.com), also Northstar Academy (www.northstar-academy.org), and also Willoway Cyber School (www.willoway.com).

If this option suits your high schooler, consider an online college education too. Students can finish college more quickly with considerably less expense. A good resource is *Accelerated Distance Learning: The New Way to Earn Your College Degree in the Twenty-First Century* by Brad Voeller (Bradley Voeller, 2001).

Part-time School

Some states, though not all, allow students to attend school for as few or as many classes as they like and homeschool the remainder. In these cases children have access to school clubs, organizations, and other resources. Get a copy of your state law, and ask around to find out if you live in a state where you can take advantage of this option. If not, don't be shy about asking around at the local private schools. Private schools are realizing that homeschooling students make good additions to their student body. They also appreciate the extra revenue brought in by these families.

Consider registering for classes at a local community college, junior college, or university as well. These schools often offer dual enrollment whereby the student applies course work to high school requirements while earning college credits.

Socializing

The inescapable *s* word continues to loom over the homeschooling movement, though very few of us worry too much about it at all. High school students may be looking for more time with friends, but hopefully they have made a handful of good ones to spend time with. Like anything else, if this is an area you find lacking, you may have to take some initiative and schedule get-togethers (movie nights, etc.) with other kids. Generally as students participate in the real world around them, they form meaningful relationships with others with whom they share common interests.

SERVICE AND WORK

All high schoolers should be actively involved in some kind of service and/or community work. It will help with any future work applications, provide them with a meaningful way to contribute to society, and also mean a lot to college admissions officers. The easiest place to look for service projects is in your church. What ministries are they involved in that a high schooler could help with? Call local organizations—candy stripers and orderlies are still needed at the hospitals, Meals on Wheels is always looking for volunteers, and various shelters and charity organizations welcome homeschoolers. Teens can volunteer at libraries, botanical gardens, literacy programs, food pantries, animal shelters, and a number of other places. You are only limited by your imagination! (See Chapter 3 of this book for further information on this important topic.)

Before your child applies for that first job, be sure you are aware of the work requirements and work laws regarding minors in your state. Work permits are not hard to obtain (check with your local homeschool group or labor and/or child services department). Some states have stricter laws than others about the hours a minor is allowed to work or at what time they must get off in the evening. However, there are a number of jobs high school students can hold. If your high schooler has too much time on his hands or is in constant need of cash (as so many high schoolers are), then by all means help him find a good job. Again, this bodes well for future job applications but also is a great tool for teaching money management before the child leaves home.

EXTRACURRICULAR ACTIVITIES

Homeschool sports teams, bands, and clubs of all kinds are growing in popularity. Because they have more time, homeschoolers are able to more fully dive into activities such as the arts, church and other ministries, scouts, and league sports. Try to form relationships with teachers and coaches who are in the best position to help your child meet his goals.

TYPICAL HIGH SCHOOL COURSE OF STUDY

Keep in mind that various states have various requirements. Prepare as advanced a course of study as you think your student is capable of. Colleges find difficult work a great preparation. The more prestigious colleges have higher standards; so be sure, if your child is interested in attending a particular school, to check out its minimum requirements ahead of time. Don't wait until it's too late.

The following is meant only to be a guide for the standard diploma. Advanced students would want to pursue more difficult studies in areas like math and science. Also, many states no longer require foreign languages, yet most colleges expect students to have taken at least some. Students who take four or five years of a foreign language (starting in the eighth grade) not only impress college admissions officers—they have a marketable life skill, can perhaps qualify for some Advanced Placement credits (by taking the AP test, see below), and will be able to fare well on a language SAT II test should their college of choice require one. Decide upon a good record-keeping system, then keep good records.

> English—four full years (a range of American and European literature should be included).
>
> History/social studies, etc.: four full years, including world history and geography, American history, American government, economics, and possibly a course in your state's history.
>
> Science—four full years, including at least biology, physics, and chemistry.
>
> Math—four full years, covering at least algebra, geometry, and algebra II.
>
> Health and physical education—two years of PE, a half-year of health.
>
> Art—one year.
>
> Computer, business—one year.

Figure the "years" as "credits," add in what is left in a standard six-period day (for four years), and then figure how many electives your student should take. Electives can be foreign language, more business and computer courses, Bible studies, art, drama, music, etc. Also, high school students should write a term paper (usually done in the junior year). While the note card system we were raised on doesn't have to be used anymore, the experience gained by choosing a topic, researching it, citing sources, outlining material, and writing a full-length research paper will serve students well when they attend college.

Spend some time perusing www.highschoolhub.org. It is a great website full of recommended reading lists, curriculum ideas for all sorts of subjects, an "SAT Question of the Day," and lots more.

Students should balance their portfolios in the same way they would want to balance their lives: academics, outside activities, work, service.

Colleges will be knocking at their door. If they want to travel or go directly into the workforce, the homeschooling life up to this time should provide ample leads to do either of those things.

COLLEGE SEARCH AND APPLICATION TIME

Few things disrupt a household as much as a young adult trying to decide which college he would like to attend and getting all the paperwork together in order to apply. Whether your child applies to one college or several, the red tape is daunting. However, it's not an insurmountable task, and many others have gone before you. There are a number of great resources out there to help, and with the World Wide Web, you can access most every college online to find out what their specific requirements are. Cathy Duffy's *Curriculum Manual* is a helpful resource. Cafi Cohen, another popular homeschooling writer and speaker, has written several helpful books, among them *And What About College?* (Holt, 2000) and *Homeschoolers' College Admission Handbook* (Prima, 2000). *Homeschooling Today* magazine produces a college issue every so often, the most recent in September/October 2002 (970-493-2716; www.homeschooltoday.com).

Transcripts/Course Requirements

If you've followed the basic course requirements recommended for high school students, you can easily put together a transcript to send off to colleges. Most colleges aren't surprised to see "homeschooler" written on an application, but you can make your transcripts look as official as you desire (samples are available in many homeschooling books). Some homeschoolers put together portfolios of samples of work, projects, awards, newspaper clippings, drawings, photos, and so on to bring with them as they visit college admission offices. These may or may not be useful, depending upon whether your college of choice encourages personal visits. Regardless, they make great keepsakes. Most colleges ask for grades and grade point averages, though those same colleges often say the standardized test scores matter more with homeschooled students. Try to demonstrate that you've completed a large body of work.

Students need to show they are well-rounded and can handle the pressure of balancing a busy life with a rigorous curriculum. Urge your child to brag as he puts together the transcripts and resumé. List places traveled to, special events attended, awards earned, groups belonged to, and anything else you think points to the student's uniqueness and leadership abilities.

Standardized Tests

The sophomore year in high school is a good year to begin studying and preparing to take standardized tests. Most colleges across the country require the SAT or ACT. Books such as *Crash Course for the SAT* and *Crash Course for the ACT* (Princeton Review, 2002) help students prepare for the tests. SAT and ACT prep courses are also available (see below for contact information). Be sure to have your child take a practice test, especially if he or she is unaccustomed to test taking. If you are associated with a covering, umbrella, or correspondence school, you will be able to tap into their resources for test preparation and test taking. Otherwise, use the library, bookstore, and Internet. Use the following list to find more information about the tests and how to sign up to take them.

> PSAT: This test is taken during the junior year in high school. The scores are used to determine National Merit finalists and semifinalists. These award winners usually receive large amounts of college scholarship money (609-771-7070; www.collegeboard.com).
> SAT and SAT II: The SAT II used to be called the Achievement Test (609-771-7600; www.collegeboard.com).
> ACT: (319-337-1270; www.act.org).

Advanced Placement tests (AP) and the College Level Examination Program (CLEP) are both avenues that allow students to earn college credit ahead of time with good test scores. Look for information on both at www.collegeboard.com; for the AP test, call 609-406-5050.

The College Essay

College applications almost always have a few essay questions for the student to answer. Applicants should take time to do a good job of writing their answers. Remember, college admission offices want a diverse student body. They aren't looking for average or run-of-the-mill. Send off for applications early, or poke around the Web and ask other homeschoolers to help you familiarize yourself with the kinds of questions you can expect to be asked. Have your student write from his or her heart, then use his or her editing skills liberally. He or she needs to show off good writing skills as well as brilliant ideas.

References

Colleges usually ask for letters of recommendation. Don't be shy about asking people to write these. You may feel like you're imposing on someone, but let me share a secret—I have recently been asked twice to write such letters, and I consider it a great privilege. It was great fun to think of all the wonderful things about these kids and just what an asset I thought they would be to the particular universities to which they applied. It was the ultimate opinion paper for me! Someone will feel the same way about writing a recommendation for your child.

NCAA Regulations

Like other requirements and regulations, the NCAA seems to be fluid when it comes to requirements of athletes. Be sure to familiarize yourself with the stringent recruiting rules. Your diligence and honesty will pay off in the long run. Many homeschoolers are college-bound athletes. Protect your student's eligibility and potential for a scholarship by knowing the rules. Put your child's coach to work for you by asking for contacts, advice, and so on. Visit www.ncaa.org, and read a book such as *Student Athlete's Guide to College* (Princeton Review, 1999) to familiarize yourself with procedures, policies, and possibilities.

Scholarships/Financial Aid

Don't limit yourself too early with preconceived notions about what your family may or may not be able to afford. Aside from the large scholarship monies offered by universities, thousands of groups offer money to candidates for a wide variety of reasons. Two of my closest friends are sending their children to large universities next fall on full scholarships. Another did the same last year. There are scholarships available to minorities, contest winners, athletes, National Merit scholars, those who can show need, and categories you would never dream possible. Also, there are a number of avenues from which to take out student loans. College admissions offices are one important source of help, but the time you spend researching on your own could pay you back in tens of thousands of dollars. Two great websites are www.fastweb.com and www.scholarship.com (both have much more than scholarship information).

During these precious high school years, your child should continue to commit him- or herself to a lifetime of learning and to make it his or her purpose to live a full, interesting, meaningful life, helping others and growing personally. What does he or she have to offer any particular college? Each child should seek to be somebody who can contribute. It is important to balance work, service, schoolwork, hobbies, arts, and athletics, to think ahead, plan, learn to handle pressure and manage time wisely, then put together an application to show the college just how he or she did so.

Shari Henry, a senior editor at Homeschooling Today *magazine, enjoys writing for various parenting and homeschooling publications. She is the author of* Homeschooling: The Middle Years: Your Complete Guide to Successfully Homeschooling the 8- to 12-Year-Old Child. *She lives in Huntsville, Alabama, with her husband, three children, and two Chocolate Labradors.*

RESOURCES

Testing Information

GED (General Educational Development exam; 800-626-9433; www.gedtest.org).

PSAT (609-771-7070; www.collegeboard.com).

SAT and SAT II (the SAT II used to be called the Achievement Test) (609-771-7600; www.collegeboard.com).

ACT (319-337-1270; www.act.org).

Books and Magazines

The Christian Home Educators' Curriculum Manual: Junior/Senior High by Cathy Duffy (Grove, 2000).

Accelerated Distance Learning: The New Way to Earn Your College Degree in the Twenty-First Century by Brad Voeller (Bradley Voeller, 2001).

And What About College? by Cafi Cohen (Holt, 2000) and *Homeschoolers' College Admission Handbook,* also by Cafi Cohen (Prima, 2000).

Crash Course for the SAT and *Crash Course for the ACT* (Princeton Review, 2002).

Student Athlete's Guide to College (Princeton Review, 1999).

Homeschooling Today magazine produces a college issue every so often, the most recent in September/October 2002 (970-493-2716; www.homeschooltoday.com).

Online Education/Helpful Websites

Bridgestar Online Academy (www.switched-onlineschoolhouse.com).

Northstar Academy (www.northstar-academy.org).

Willoway Cyber School (www.willoway.com).

highschoolhub.org—a great website full of recommended reading lists, curriculum ideas for all sorts of subjects, an "SAT Question of the Day," and lots more.

www.ncaa.org

Online Scholarship/Financial Aid Information

www.fastweb.com

www.scholarship.com

5

WORKING WITH
TRADITIONAL SCHOOLS

Our children attended public school prior to being homeschooled. Our local elementary school was directly across the street from our home. Our front door faced their front door. I was a former teacher in that community and knew many of the teachers at that school. I even spent a year as a substitute teacher there. I was quite involved. I was on the PTA board, produced the school's newsletter, had a seat on the school's advisory council, and was on a first-name basis with many of the faculty and staff. When we brought our children home to school, I wanted to maintain those relationships. I still wanted the boys to participate in certain school classes and activities. It is a neighborhood school in a close-knit community. I didn't want to lose that feeling of community. I also didn't know what the future would bring. What if I decided to put them back in school at some point?

BUILD BRIDGES—DON'T BURN THEM

Even if your children never attended a public school, it is still in everyone's best interest to cultivate positive relationships with your neighborhood schools. Teachers and school personnel in general do not know enough homeschoolers personally to form a positive opinion about homeschooling. Even though homeschooling is now mainstream, it still seems like a mysterious phenomenon to most educators. The only way to be a "sweet aroma" (2 Corinthians 2:14, NASB) to them is by first being visible.

Even if you pulled your child from a public school because of a negative experience, it is still up to you to promote a positive image of homeschoolers. You might argue that you are not in the public relations business and therefore feel no responsibility to cultivate any relationship with the public schools. However, as a Christian homeschooler—the biggest group of homeschoolers in this country—you do have a responsibility to represent Christ to those around you. Since most public educators and the media believe that most parents homeschool for religious reasons, it is God's reputation on the line if you put forth a negative or adversarial image of homeschoolers.

If your child had a detrimental experience in a public school, you might consider the school an "enemy." How are we to treat our enemies? When we pulled our sons from their elementary school, it was after three years of struggling to get my oldest son's needs met. Finally the principal said to me, "Vicki, I guess we can't help you here. I can't make my teachers do something they don't want to do." That was devastating to hear, especially being a teacher myself. I knew what they could do—they just chose not to do it. Even though that was heartbreaking, I continued to produce the school's newsletter and remained on the school advisory council. My children attended gifted classes there one day per week. It was still our neighborhood school, and I wanted to help make it a better place for all children who attend. As a result, the principal opened his doors to any homeschooler who wanted to participate in any classes or activities at the school. We were all part of the same community. We were there to serve one another's needs.

God calls us to a higher standard than those who do not belong to Him. Even if other homeschoolers think you are "diluting the movement" by participating in something sponsored by a public school, you can and should do what is best for your children. Even if the school's principal has had a negative experience with homeschoolers in the past, you can show him that not all homeschoolers are alike. After all, that is indeed true about teachers and schools—they are not all alike. If we focus instead on the relationship, we can both win.

EDUCATIONAL CONSUMERISM

In the wake of school vouchers and other accountability measures, all parents of school-age children have a stronger offer of choice than ever before—and they're taking advantage of it! Unfortunately, educational philosophers and writers are worried about the new consumer mentality toward education. Picking and choosing what is best for your child somehow threatens some of the fundamental beliefs about public education. Homeschooling is now seen as one more anomaly of consumerism. Is it a good thing that people can now choose what education they want for their children? Of course it is! But in a system whose wheels turn slower than almost any other institution, the watchdogs of public education are dismayed at this current trend.

As homeschoolers, this trend toward consumerism only makes it easier to partner with public schools if that is what you desire. Catering toward the needs of individual students is found throughout the professional literature. This is a concept whose time has finally come. How blessed we are to have these choices! If you choose to engage in public school classes or activities, that is your right as a parent. Be aware, however, that many watchdogs of the homeschooling movement are just as unhappy with you for pursuing a relationship with the public schools as the watchdogs of public education are. But they are your children, and it is your choice!

WHAT TRADITIONAL SCHOOLS HAVE TO OFFER

• *Individual classes*: In most states homeschoolers are permitted to enroll in one or more individual classes. Many homeschoolers are grateful for this option, especially during the high school years for classes like biology or chemistry, which both require labs. Other classes are available as well. Inquire at your local school district's office for more information.

• *Part-time enrollment (or dual enrollment)*: In many areas you can take up to half the amount of classes at the public school for credit. Part-time enrollment may only be available on a case by case basis in some areas.

• *Testing*: As discussed in the chapter on testing and evaluation, homeschoolers can take the required standardized test at their zoned school. It's free, and it gives your child an opportunity to get used to that type of testing environment if that is important to you.

• *Homeschool enrichment classes*: Little by little, public school districts are going out of their way to offer enrichment classes for homeschoolers. Sometimes they create an enrichment program housed in a school whose enrollment is low. Sometimes they use charter schools to offer "cottage" schools for homeschoolers. The classes are taught by certified teachers who may or may not be homeschoolers, and therefore there is usually no cost.

• *Athletics and extracurricular activities*: Many states' statutes specify how homeschoolers can participate in school athletics. Check with your district for details.

• *Special education services*: If your child is tested through the school system and qualifies for a particular service, that system is obligated to serve your child if you so choose. The testing is free, but you usually need to dual enroll in the school first. That doesn't mean your child must attend the school, but on paper your child will be counted as a student and will be assigned a student number. That number is required before testing can be administered. Keep in mind that there is usually a waiting list for testing, even for those children who already attend that school.

• *Regular diploma*: Different districts may offer different diploma options. Here in Colorado Springs, if I want my son to receive a regular diploma at the end of high school, he is required to spend his senior year full-time at a high school of my choice. For some students this is a great opportunity, especially if Mom doesn't want the responsibility of documenting credits and preparing a transcript. It also gives the student a chance to begin to make a transition away from home and into the world. College shouldn't be your child's first independent experience of being accountable to organize and complete his schooling.

SCHOOL CULTURE

A school is unlike any other place to work or interact. It has its own culture with its own language, customs, rules, ceremonies, and power-holders. Just as you would find out more about the culture of another country and try to learn some of its language before you travel there, it is highly recommended to do the same preparation if you are not familiar with a particular school's culture. How you experienced it as a student yourself is different than how you will experience it as an adult. Your child will have to learn and conform to some procedures and customs on his own, but your interaction as a parent will speak volumes.

• *Language*: Some people refer to this as *educationese*. It often consists of abbreviations and acronyms (i.e., IEP, DALT testing, SAC, and other organizational and testing titles). The key to understanding the language at least well enough to understand how it affects your child is immersion. Spend time at the school, and talk to teachers with whom you volunteer. Ask questions. Let them know you really want to understand.

• *Customs*: Checking in at the front office when you visit, utilizing the established way to communicate with teachers (phone, e-mail, etc.), scheduling conferences instead of just dropping by to talk about Johnny, looking through your child's backpack for written communication (sometimes things go home every day!), and sending back in a timely manner anything you are asked to sign are some of the unique customs in a school. Doing things your way instead only shows disrespect and leads to strife. If you want to have an enjoyable experience at this school, follow its customs.

• *Power-holders*: Every school has a principal, but the principal is not the only power-holder in a school. The principal's secretary or the front office secretary (depending upon the size of your school) has a great deal of power. Never try to circumvent any of them. There is a chain of command to follow—follow it! It is also highly recommended to go to the teacher first if you have a problem. Never go over his or her head. Not only will the teacher be hurt, the principal will not look favorably on your action. The lunchroom manager is also a person of power. Encourage your child to be respectful and pleasant whenever he or she interacts with food service personnel. Every year I send some sort of baked goodies to the lunchroom staff to thank them for taking care of our children. My mother was a lunch lady, so I know it is appreciated.

• *Ceremonies*: School is a place of ceremony. There are many reasons to either celebrate or commemorate during the school year. Participating in these ceremonies and celebrations brings the school together as a community. If your child only attends school for a small portion of the week, he or she can still feel a part of it if you make an effort to attend some of these functions. As a parent, you will feel more comfortable as well instead of feeling like someone who just drops off and picks up.

• *Rules*: Schools also have rules. I'm sure you remember that from your own experience. Make sure you and your child review the "Welcome to Our School" packet when you register. It will outline the school rules and disciplinary actions. You cannot claim ignorance, especially if you received notice of the rules. But just as when you travel it is your responsibility to educate yourself as to the rules and regulations of the other country, once you make the decision to participate in a traditional public school, you are under the authority of that school.

When my youngest went to a homeschool enrichment program at a local elementary school, he had a slight sore throat one week. I sent him to school with vitamin C drops to soothe and moisten it. The principal called me that same morning informing me that any medication (even over-the-counter throat drops) must be checked into the office along with a form authorizing the school to administer the treatment. It was out of my own ignorance that this happened. The principal was quite gracious and did not scold me or my child, but my son felt badly when his teacher told him to take the drops to the principal. Whether or not you agree with the rules is besides the point. As long as they are not asking us or our children to sin, we must submit to their authority.

WHAT YOU HAVE TO OFFER SCHOOLS

We tend to look at involvement in traditional schools in a one-sided manner. *What can the school do for my child? What will we get out of it?* I would like to challenge you to consider what you might add or bring to that school. *What can you give?* Any formal participation in a school gives the school more funding based on head count, but more than that, your child can be a light to other children and even teachers. We can offer school staff a positive image of homeschoolers. We can support their efforts to teach all children (a thankless and difficult job). We can offer our services as volunteers. We can supplement the classroom experience if we are an expert in some area that they are studying.

Often public schools are dismayed about homeschooling because they think they are losing families that really care about education and are involved. More than once teachers have said to me, "You're just the kind of parent we need at this school. Your children are just the kind of children we need to encourage us in our quest as teachers." We can change the image of homeschoolers from an elitist, isolationist, fanatical group of disgruntled parents to a caring, involved, quality-minded group of responsible parents.

Top Ten Tips for Working with Traditional Schools

• *Choose wisely.* In many areas choice is the way schools do business. If you have a choice, then make the effort to research the class or program in which your child wants to participate, visit the school and observe the classroom, talk to other parents whose children also attend this class or program, and ask questions. Find out what you need to find out before making such a commitment for your child.

• *Find out about and follow the rules.* As stated earlier in this chapter, schools have rules. If you did not receive them in writing, ask for them. Each teacher may also have his or her own rules in addition to the general school rules. Make sure your child understands what is expected of him or her.

• *Be visible.* Most likely you will drive your child to this school for whatever class or activity you've chosen. Once in a while, park the car and walk in with your child. Greet the teacher. Instead of sending in a note with your child for his teacher, walk into the office and ask the secretary to please put it in the teacher's mailbox. This way she will recognize you the next time you enter the building.

• *Be supportive.* No teachers want to do a bad job. Usually they chose teaching because they love children and want to make a positive impact. But teachers are people too. They are moms, dads, husbands, and wives. They get tired. They get frustrated. They can go through a personal crisis and not be as responsive to your child as you would like. What can you do to encourage your child's teacher?

• *Be on time.* Sometimes homeschoolers have a reputation of not taking the school schedule or calendar seriously. Don't get into a habit of being late or skipping class in favor of another activity. Just because your child is not enrolled full-time in the school doesn't mean you should take the school's expectations any less seriously.

• *Be committed.* Public school classes, activities, or programs are available to homeschoolers only if there is room. Preference is given to those already attending the school full-time. Take your child's placement in a class seriously, realizing that it is not a "I'll go when I feel like it" class. If the class or activity spans the entire school year, commit to the entire school year. If you are not sure you are willing to make such a commitment, then don't participate. Let someone else have that space who will commit to being there and will take it seriously. This is a chance to model and teach strong character traits.

• *Be respectful.* Sometimes students who have been primarily homeschooled take offense when things don't go their way in a school setting. They're not used to the variety of personalities, rules, and temperaments of different teachers. If things aren't done the way Mom does them at home, they may voice their disappointment or disapproval aloud to their teacher. They may come home complaining about how the teacher does this or that. School is not meant to be the same as home. Model and teach your children tolerance, compassion, and patience while at school. Personalities may clash, but it is still up to our children to submit to this authority placed in their lives. Make sure you always speak respectfully to or about your child's teacher. If your child speaks disrespectfully to or about his or her teacher, which may be an indicator of an attitude of defiance, nip it in the bud. One of the greatest complaints of teachers is that children speak disrespectfully to them in school. This is a heartbreaker.

• *Participate.* Schools make a great effort to involve parents in the process. Even if your child only attends school for one class, look for ways to become involved. Can you chaperone on a field trip? Can you bake something for a class party? Whatever you do, try not to adopt that drop off/pick up mentality. Conversely, don't overstep your bounds as a parent and become meddlesome. Let the teachers do their job and teach.

• *Form relationships.* A teacher has a relationship with your child; so it stands to reason that as parents we should be in relationship with the teachers. We want teachers to get to know our children well enough to meet their needs. Try to get to know their teachers well enough to recognize *their* needs. This might mean friendship. It might mean helping in the classroom. It might mean saying a kind word at just the right time. Parents and teachers need to be in partnership for the sake of the children.

• *Be humble.* Home is our domain, not school. Remember not to act as if you know better when it comes to dealing with the school. Teachers can be territorial, and an attitude of arrogance on your part will not make your child's learning environment a pleasant place to be. Defer to their judgment. Try not to tell them how or what to teach. If you are not ready to lose some control over your child's education, school may not be the right place for him or her yet.

There are many ways to become involved in traditional schools as homeschoolers. Your reasons to do so are your own. Just as a Christian is called to live *in* the world but not *of* it, we can be in the public schools but not of them. Our initial reasons to be in the schools all involve securing a quality education for our children, but the consequences of our participation reach further than our own families. We can promote a positive image of homeschooling. We can build bridges of community. And most importantly, we can let God show them who He is through us.

RESOURCES

Helping Your Child Succeed in Public School by Cheri Fuller (Focus on the Family, 1999).

6

Homeschooling in the Military

By Ellie Kay

We were lost on a country road in northern New York. However, we weren't *so* lost that Bob felt the need to ask for directions. After all, we'd only been lost, driving aimlessly with five, squirming, hungry children for about *two hours*. My beloved has to be lost for about *three hours* and down to a gallon of gas in the tank before he feels it's finally time to ask for directions. Of course, that leaves me praying with all the fervency I can muster that we won't run out of gas before we find a station.

I don't understand my husband's sense of direction sometimes. I mean, when he's in his Stealth F-117 jet, he can find a target the size of a postage stamp, but in our car he misses the turnoff for the rural road we're supposed to take. I just don't understand him. I'm not like that. I can follow and give *great* directions.

For example, if you were coming to my house, I would first find out where you're coming from. Are you coming from the mountain side of Alamogordo or the flat side? (Don't you hate it the way men always ask for that north and south stuff?)

If you're coming from the mountain side, then you just take the highway that leads into town. (I can't remember the name of it, but it comes into town from the mountain side.) That highway will turn into a street that will go right by the White Sands Mall. Every woman knows that malls are the best landmarks in the whole town. If you get lost, you can always shop.

The mall should be on your right, I mean your left—you know, the *other* right. Go past the mall until you see a small zoo on your right. If you see the zoo, you know you're going the right direction. Then you go to the

Kentucky Fried Chicken. (Restaurants are the second-best landmarks because you can snack along the way if you get turned around.) Take a left at the KFC, which will be on your right. You know, the *other* right.

The road will go by a pretty white house with red-and-white checkered curtains and yellow flowers in the flower bed (unless it's in the fall; then the flowers won't be there). Just keep going. If you get to the golf course, you've gone too far, and you're on the wrong side of town. Then you'll come to a house with a bunch of plastic ducks out front; turn right at that road. We are the second house on the right, unless you count the first house, which is really on the other street because we are kind of on the intersection. If you count it that way, then we're the first house on the right. No, the *other* right.

You can't miss our house. It's a two-story. Actually, there are lots of two-story houses on our road. But ours is the one with the Americana style wreath on the front door and a garden in the backyard. Of course, you can't see the garden from the road, but it's there nonetheless. Our house is real easy to find—you can't miss it. But bring your cell phone just in case you get lost.

I just can't understand why Bob gets lost, especially when I'm giving him directions.

As a military family, we've spent lots of time asking for directions for two basic reasons: 1) We've moved twelve times in fourteen years, and 2) it seems we're always living someplace new and unfamiliar. Moving is only one of the challenges that military families face. And when a move is involved, the family must again consider the all-important decision about their children's education. We made the decision to homeschool our kids for four main reasons. The majority of these reasons are common among military families. I'll go into greater depth with each of these topics later in the chapter, but the primary reasons for homeschooling were:

• *Frequent moves.* In our case, we moved frequently. With one assignment, we were only there for three months! We opted to homeschool in order to give our children continuity in their lives.

• *Quality of education.* The second reason we homeschooled was found in the quality of the state education. When we moved to one state (ranked 49th in the nation), other military families told us that our kids would be way behind if we sent them to public school. We didn't want to move from that state only to discover that our child was now two years behind his classmates in our new home.

• *Cost factors.* As a young military family with lots of kids at home and two older children in college, we couldn't afford the tuition of a private school. We also had forty thousand dollars of consumer debt when we got married—the result of bad choices. We were essentially living on the equivalent of a young airman even though Bob was a captain.

• *Individual needs.* The final reason we chose this education option was because one of our sons was a slow reader at that time. He was in the third grade and barely reading on a kindergarten level. We were concerned that he would be left behind in a conventional classroom. Once his language skills kicked in, he regained three years of reading ability in six months, but at that time he was still struggling.

FREQUENT MOVES

When we were moving from Holloman Air Force Base in New Mexico to Fort Drum in northern New York, it took seven days to make the trip. One morning we were trying to get the five children, ranging in ages from two to nine, ready for the day's journey. I usually packed sandwiches for lunch, but we were already behind schedule, and I was running out of time. The older children scrambled to get their toys, coloring books, pillows, and travel games into the already stuffed Suburban. As I carried three-year-old Jonathan to his car seat, I called out to Bob, who was strapping two-year-old Joshua into his seat, "Bob, don't worry about lunches, we'll just eat on the road." Immediately Jonathan began to cry.

"What's wrong, precious?" I asked him as I stroked his face, convinced that moving was sometimes harder on children than on parents.

He looked up at me with his big, hazel eyes surrounded by thick, black lashes and whimpered, "But if we eat on de road, we might get runned ober by a car!"

Poor Jonathan didn't understand what it meant to "eat on the road," but he did make an interesting point. When you're moving as often as you do in the military, it's important to plan ahead so you won't get "runned ober" by the sheer demands of moving and homeschooling. Once you find out where you will be assigned, there are quite a few things that you will want to do ahead of time to prepare for your child's education in the new location. Some of these practical services are at your fingertips, and you may not even realize it. The following is a checklist that you can follow before (and shortly after) each PCS (permanent change of station.) They also serve as a great resource, even if you're already settled.

• *Sponsorship programs.* Most military families are part of a sponsorship program when they move to a new area. That is, an incoming family is assigned a sponsor who helps them make the transition to the new installation. If you do not have a sponsor, then have the active duty member ask his supervisor for one. The sponsors can send a package of information that they receive at the local Family Support Center or Army Community Services center. This package will include information about public, DOD (Department of Defense), and private schools. It will sometimes even offer the point of contact for a homeschool organization on base.

• *SITES (Standard Installation Topic Exchange System)*. This is another program offered through the transition assistance office (usually found in the Family Support Center). If you request one of these packages on the new installation, it will have all the educational information you will need. Besides that, these packages offer a wide variety of information about extracurricular activities that could end up being part of your home-school curriculum. This might include sports information (basketball, soccer, swimming, and baseball offered on post), youth lessons that may be offered on-site (our kids took cross-country skiing when we were stationed at Fort Drum), information on local museums, and cultural opportunities.

• *HSLDA*. Every military family should be part of the Home School Legal Defense Association (HSLDA). This organization can be found at www.hslda.org or you can write them at P.O. Box 3000, Purcellville, VA 20134-9000; phone: 540-338-5600; fax: 540-338-2733; e-mail: info@hslda.org. The HSLDA website has a great amount of information that can help you with your homeschooling needs in the area to which you are moving. With your membership in this organization you have legal representation whenever social services or the local government decides to knock on your door and ask why your kids aren't in "school." We were members each year we homeschooled and found that the brotherhood of more than seventy thousand families was a great resource for us. HSLDA also kept us current on state legislation and education requirements as we moved from state to state (and even overseas.)

• *Installation requirements*. If you live in military housing, there could be additional required paperwork that you will need to file in order to homeschool your children. These requirements change from year to year; so it's best to contact your Family Support Center or its equivalent to get printed information on these requirements. This is something else you could ask your sponsor to get for you.

• *Room for school*. Most military housing is known to be quite small when compared to civilian housing. However, some installations have spacious older homes that make a great environment for schooling your child. If you can put two children in one room in order to have a separate room for schooling, I'd encourage you to consider that as an option. Or you could even be a bit creative. In one home we took the dining room, which had a separate patio door and was off the kitchen, and made it into our schoolroom. This "great room" was long enough to accommodate our den and dining room set, and the arrangement worked well. At another assignment, we took the back den and used it as a schoolroom, once again combining the dining room and den into the same area.

But the best resource I've ever seen on how to organize your space is the book *The Organized Homeschooler* by Vicki Caruana (Crossway Books, 2001). It helps you find space in non-spacious military housing.

QUALITY OF EDUCATION

Bob had just become a commander of an aerial targets squadron and was having fun playing with the ultimate remote control airplane—a F-106 fighter jet. We decided to invite one of his men to dinner along with his new wife. No sooner had the major and his wife been seated than we realized we weren't going to be serving roast beast at dinner as we had planned. Instead, we were going to open a can of worms. The major's wife asked the children, "Where do you go to school?"

Seven-year-old Philip replied, "We're homeschooled by my mama, and we love it!"

The major's wife almost choked on her asparagus. "What? You don't go to school?"

"Yes, we do," nine-year-old Daniel interjected with a wisdom uncommon to his years. "We go to school. It's just that my mom is the teacher."

"Well," she said with an I'm-an-authority-on-the-subject-just-ask-me look, "I'm halfway through my associate degree in education, and I don't believe that homeschooling gives children the socialization they need. I assume that most parents who would do that to their children are uninformed about these needs in children."

The dinner went downhill from there.

That major's wife wasn't nearly as informed as she pretended to be. If she had done her homework, she would have discovered that homeschooled kids consistently perform better on standardized tests than children who attend public school. The one-on-one interaction between parent and child is a fabulous way to help kids learn! But our aggressive dinner guest did make one point rather well: Whether the classroom is located in the living room or in the local elementary school, the *quality* of a child's education is what matters most. Here are a few things to consider when we look at the quality of education in our part of the world.

• *State rankings.* As I mentioned earlier, if there is a deficiency in the quality of education offered in the public school arena, that greatly increases the desire for a family to homeschool their children. SITES packages will sometimes list the state's educational ranking. If not, you can contact the superintendent of schools (listed in the SITES brochure) and find out the state's ranking.

• *DOD schools.* Some installations have DOD (Department of Defense) schools that offer the added benefit of accountability to parents because most military parents tend to be very responsive and involved when their kids are in a DOD school. However, you also have to consider the fact that the curriculum may be inconsistent with your religious and personal beliefs.

• *Homeschool support groups.* Sometimes there's a support group located right on your military installation. To find out if one exists, contact the Family Support Center or Army Community Services. Almost every community now has these support groups; so if they do not exist on your base, then contact the group downtown. There are also statewide support groups that take your homeschooling experience to the next level through their conventions and planned interactive events. Local groups offer a wide variety of services and benefits, depending upon the size and focus of the group.

We were in a support group in Colorado Springs that had a college science professor (one of the moms) who gave a weekly class to our children. Almost every imaginable class is offered through some of these groups, but you have to see what is offered in your local area. Besides classes, these groups also provide a sense of camaraderie for your children. They realize that they are not alone in this educational choice, and in a group environment they receive the socialization (the number one complaint of homeschooling critics).

Some final benefits of homeschooling support groups are the ability to participate in graduation ceremonies (kindergarten, eighth grade, and high school), field trips, science fairs, orchestras, bands, sports teams, spelling bees, geography bees, SAT prep classes, and forensic debates. The military homeschooling support group on a base would also provide support for the unique needs of military families to include an understanding of deployments, TDYs (Temporary Duty assignments), training exercises, and even the challenges associated with sending a loved one to war.

Before you move. There are a few other practical considerations for the military homeschooling family to consider as they are actually packing for a move. Since arrival times of household goods can be somewhat unpredictable, be sure you pull out all the books, supplies, and materials you will need for school—even if it is a summer move. You don't want your baggage to be in Timbuktu when school starts for the year. This is especially true if you are moving overseas and have hold baggage to pack. Even though the weight limit is very precious and books can be heavy, it's wise to prioritize this for your move in the event your baggage delivery is delayed.

Timing on moves. One of the wonderful benefits of a homeschooling family is the flexibility in schedule. In order to minimize the already stressful environment associated with a move, try to schedule time off from school for this event. Or incorporate some of the cross-country sights into your curriculum. As soon as you receive that new assignment, consider the timing for your school and plan accordingly.

COST FACTORS

My children have grown up as the "Coupon Kids"—what else would you expect from the offspring of "The Savings Queen"? It was a game for my kids to locate desired items and figure out what the price would be after the double-coupon savings. They learned math while helping me shop.

One day seven-year-old Bethany innocently asked, "Mama, would you say I'm a 'Coupon Princess'?" She had long had a fascination with the idea of royalty, especially after she saw on television the homemade tiara that I sometimes wore as a sight gag. She loved the idea of her mama being a "Queen" when it came to saving money.

I looked at my blonde-haired, blue-eyed cherub. "Why *yes*, Bethany, I'd say you're a 'Coupon Princess.'"

She looked at me seriously. "Then can I have your crown when you die?"

There was no doubt that Bethany coveted my rhinestone tiara, but she was also learning the value of saving money. One of the reasons we homeschooled was to save money; the cost of private education was beyond our reach in those early years. Cost factors were definitely involved in our decision to homeschool our children. However, you should be aware that homeschooling your children involves a certain level of financial commitment—it's definitely not a free ride! This can be a problem for some military families.

For many years, younger military troops in the enlisted pay bracket would end up going into harm's way with a military pay (considering the hours worked) equivalent to a minimum-wage job at McDonald's. There was something radically wrong with that picture. Here are some updates on programs for military families as well as some practical ways to cut costs for homeschoolers.

• *FSSA and government assistance programs.* Those of us in the military know there's a need for articulate, experienced voices who will speak up on behalf of pay increases for military members. But with the recent Family Supplemental Subsistence Allowance (FSSA) act about a year ago, the need for military members to be on government assistance (food stamps) has been eliminated. If your family qualifies for food stamps, you qualify for the FSSA, which is included in your pay. Once you receive the FSSA, you're no longer eligible for food stamps. WIC (Women, Infants, and Children) is another program available to military families, but while income is a prime factor for that program, it isn't the only factor. I'd recommend that you take advantage of these resources if your family qualifies.

• *Military financial aid assistance.* Each branch of the service has a military program designed to meet the unique financial needs of military families. The Air Force Aid Society, The Fleet and Family Support Center (Navy and Marines), and the Army Emergency Relief Fund are all available to help families with needs, subject to certain criteria.

• *Military family agencies.* Two primary organizations lobby for the rights of military families independently from the services offered by each branch of the service. You might want to check them out and see where you could benefit from the vast number of programs; contact information is posted on their websites. These are: National Military Family Association, at www.NMFA.org and the Military Child Education Coalition, at www.militarychild.org.

• *Used curriculum.* If you decide you're going to homeschool on your next assignment, or if you already are homeschooling, then contact your local homeschool support group and ask them when they are having their used curriculum swap/sale. If they do not have one, then consider putting one together. The best time to do this is in March or April, so homeschool teachers will have adequate time to order the materials they couldn't pick up used.

The main thing to keep in mind with used curriculum is: Will it meet your homeschool needs; can you make it work for you? What good is a textbook if the student workbook is out-of-print and you can't order it? This means you would have to develop your own workbook. If you have time to do that, then this could work for you. However, it could require many, many hours to develop such a workbook. Homeschooling is enough of a challenge without adding these additional tasks. You have to carefully consider the financial and time trade-offs when purchasing used curriculum.

Another way to get used curriculum is to swap with another family who has the books you will need for the following year. Some families swap other items for books, such as household goods or clothing, turning the swap into a win/win situation.

• *New curriculum fairs.* It is very important to not duplicate curriculum or purchase materials that will not work for your homeschool. This is a waste of money and one area where homeschoolers are likely to blow their budgets.

If you can go to a curriculum fair in which several distributors are participating, it would be worth the trip. *Before* the fair, try to get catalogs from the major distributors (call the toll-free operator at 800-555-1212 and ask for the curriculum company's phone number). Or conduct a search for the company online, and look over their products at that time.

Do your homework by looking over the catalogs and writing down the materials you would like to order for the coming year. Pay attention to which textbooks/lesson plans/teacher's guides/quiz keys you need to review in person at the curriculum fair, and indicate these on your list with an asterisk.

The reason you want to look at some of these resources is because you may not need to order the lesson plans if the materials seem to be self-explanatory. If you have a good grasp of mathematics, for example, then you may already know how to teach addition and won't need the teacher guide for first grade. I didn't really need these additional resources until my children were in the second and third grade, depending upon the subject. On the other hand, I learned very quickly, when my oldest was in the third grade, that a mathematics workbook teacher's key was worth nine dollars a year, so I wouldn't have to do each and every fraction and long division problem.

If you are not yet confident in teaching your children at home, you might feel better ordering the full curriculum. If you are more experienced or have a good grasp of teaching, then you can avoid purchasing a lot of materials without compromising the integrity of the material your child is learning.

• *Postage and handling.* When you order from a curriculum fair or a special demonstration set up in the local area (usually in hotel conference rooms or churches), you can oftentimes avoid sales tax and postage and handling fees. Be sure to ask about these special offers before ordering your materials.

• *Multiple children.* If you have more than one child and know you will homeschool them for more years, you may want to pay special attention to "last edition" indicators in your favorite catalog. The curriculum providers usually indicate in their catalogs when they are revising the curriculum. If you already have a teacher's guide/key/lesson plan text, you might want to consider ordering additional student workbooks for your younger children as well. You might have to pay a little more this year, but it saves the expensive cost of teacher's curriculum for next year (and possibly the year after).

When you are schooling many children, think in terms of investment. I ordered A Beka Bible teaching aids for a variety of series and topics and taught those subjects to all of the children at once. They were good investments in terms of time and money. They can also be used outside of homeschooling for Sunday school classes or neighborhood summer Bible clubs. Learn to think in terms of investment whether you're ordering teaching equipment, desks, curriculum, or supplies.

• *Sharing your used curriculum.* Jessica, a homeschooling friend of mine, schooled two children all the way through high school. Her children are now young adults of whom she is quite proud. She said that when she completed her youngest child's curriculum, she always looked for a family that could use it and *gave* it to them. Jessica also found that when she practiced giving these things away, God always provided enough money to buy the next year's curriculum. Sometimes someone else provided her needs by giving her the textbooks she needed to teach her children.

• *Library resources.* Some of my friends used the library for the majority of their curriculum, but there are limitations to this approach. For one thing, there's far more planning, organizing, and research involved in this approach. The homeschool teacher will have to have an extra ten hours a week (approximately, depending upon your organizational skills) in order to take advantage of this approach for the *majority* of the curriculum needs. When a spouse is deployed for training or even for war, this is a good way to productively fill the time at home, but that must be balanced by the fact that a deployed spouse leaves a gap. Sometimes this gap is filled with added stress, and you may not want the pressure of the additional preparation involved in this approach.

The base library and even some installation youth centers offer free access to computers, readers, and resources for book reports and research papers. Your child can also request information from other libraries via an interlibrary loan. There are also computer programs that access thousands of periodicals for research information.

INDIVIDUAL NEEDS

The base was conducting an exercise alternating the security requirements between Threatcon Bravo and the more serious Threatcon Charlie. Just as any able-minded person wouldn't dare make jokes about guns and bombs while walking through metal detectors at an airport, you wouldn't make jokes when going through the base security check at the main gate—especially during a Threatcon Charlie exercise. But Myra wasn't really able-minded: Her husband had deployed for the eighth time in six months, and she was fending off three very cute (but *very active)* preschoolers. So she's not responsible for what she did at the gate. If it were a court of law, I'm sure any jury would declare her to be temporarily insane after seven straight nights of nursing sick kids with colds and ear infections.

At any rate, Myra drove up to the security gate in a squeaky clean van—she'd just been through the car wash for the third time in three days. It seems that Hunter, her three-year-old son, found life's fulfillment by going through the small town's brand-new automatic, handy-dandy, triple deluxe wash system—with colored bubbles, no less! (Who says marketing researchers didn't know how many minivans they could clean with that sly tactic?) Every time Myra would drive by the facility (which happened to be several times a day because it was on the main drag in town), Hunter would announce from his car seat, "Car deedy, Mama!"

Just in case Mama hadn't heard how dirty he thought the car was, he'd shout it again. "Car deedy, Mama!"

On the day in question, Myra ignored him and drove her daughter to school.

"Car deedy, Mama!"

She went by the drive-in cleaners and pulled out her credit card.

"Car deedy, Mama!"

She pulled into the drive-through bank. He yelled into the teller's microphone, "Car deedy, Mama!"

Moms are good at ignoring kids for a remarkably long time. But any mom who is honest will tell you that it begins to wear on you about the thirty-second time.

"Car deedy, Mama!"

Hunter was no quitter. But Myra was—especially when she was doing the single mom thing.

"Car deedy, Mama!"

Much to Hunter's delight, his life was once again fulfilled for the day as he giggled and shouted over the colorful bubbles. Their van was squeaky clean as she drove by the security forces guard at the gate during Threatcon Charlie.

The young airman sported an M-16 on his back as he approached Myra's open window. He wore his Battle Dress Uniform (BDUS), which was especially hot on this sweltering day in the New Mexico desert. He was in no joking mood.

Myna was so relieved that she had a temporary respite from Hunter's endless chattering. She absentmindedly pulled her identification out of her wallet for the guard who now stood in front of her window.

"Ma'am, we are in Threatcon Charlie. May I see your military identification?"

Myra smiled smugly at her efficiency (who says mothers of young children don't have it together?). She had the card ready; the guard wouldn't
have to tap his foot impatiently while she searched for it in her purse.

She thrust it through the window so the policeman could see it clearly.

He looked shocked at first, eyeing Myra suspiciously. Then he took
one look at sleeping baby Holly and glanced over at Hunter in his car seat
(who was, once again, shouting you-know-what).

For the first time that day he smiled.

"Well, ma'am, that's a really nice *credit card*, but I'll need to see some
other ID."

Myra is a smart woman, but she was also a stressed woman thanks
to everything that was happening in her life at the time. She and her kids
make sacrifices, just as all military families do, for what their spouse does
to defend our nation's freedoms. While the military spouse and their children won't likely get a medal for their role in our nation's defense, I believe
the argument can be made that they deserve one. If you are reading this
and you're a military spouse, you need to know that you are a hero too
because of your contribution to the military member's stability. When
things are taken care of at home, the soldier, airman, or sailor is able to
concentrate more fully on his or her task both at home and abroad. You're
a hidden hero—the hero at home.

While the military lifestyle is filled with adventure and excitement, it
can also be stressful due to the family separations and other pressures that
accompany that life. This final section will help you evaluate the individual needs of your child and family situation and your ability to homeschool.

For example, if you are attempting to homeschool for the first time at
the same time that your spouse is deployed for a one-year unaccompanied
remote or hardship tour, you will need to count the cost of what this venture will entail. Here are a few ideas that can help you decide, on an annual
basis, whether the homeschool option is the best choice for your military
year.

• *Stress factors*. The top-ranking stress factors, besides the death of a
spouse, include events that regularly occur in the lives of military families.
Some of the top ten include: separation from spouse, moves, birth of a
baby, geographical separation from extended family, health issues, change
(or loss) of jobs, and new schools.

One of the reasons we decided to homeschool was to give the children
continuity for military moves and to provide consistency in light of their

dad's frequent TDYs and deployments. However, while this may have been a good choice for us, each person is wired differently. When a spouse is deployed, it may cause more stress for the remaining spouse to undertake the monumental work of homeschooling.

I would encourage you to list all the stress factors involved in your upcoming academic year, and list these as pros and cons on a sheet of paper. Sit down with your spouse, and prayerfully consider the options that are available to you.

• *Individual choice.* Once we were in a financial position to afford private education, and when we considered the pressures I had in a developing writing and speaking career, we decided on a different educational route. However, each and every year we evaluate our children's needs as well as our own abilities and time constraints. A good resource for this ongoing decision is *Success in School* by Vicki Caruana (Focus Publishing, 1999).

• *Peer pressure.* We lived in military housing for the first twelve moves in Bob's military career. Some bases were more conducive and supportive of homeschooling than others. While we received criticism, such as the incident I mentioned with the major's wife, we also received support for our educational choice. Whether you find yourself surrounded by positive or negative peer pressure, it's important to seek out the support of other like-minded families.

Whatever you decide to do, make sure you include your spouse and children in the decision-making process. Also, make sure you have taken adequate time to consider all aspects of homeschooling—from finances, to time constraints, to your own personality bent. You'll feel better about your decision if it's an intelligent, informed decision, made with the blessing of both your family and God.

Ellie Kay is the wife of (in her words) "The World's Greatest Fighter Pilot" and mother to five school-age and two adult children. She's the best-selling author of seven books including Money Doesn't Grow on Trees: Teaching Kids the Value of a Buck *(Bethany House Publishers).*

7

SUPPORT GROUPS AND CO-OPS

This is the best time to homeschool. There are so many curriculum choices, so many enrichment opportunities, and more support than ever before. You don't have to go it alone, unless you make it a point to do so. The first year we homeschooled, I didn't venture out very often. It was overwhelming enough just trying to figure out what we were doing. By the end of the first year I found myself crying quite often. I felt very alone and wondered if the isolation of homeschooling was too high of a cost. I knew about our area support groups, but I didn't know anyone and felt uncomfortable attending a meeting. But when the beginning of the next school loomed in front of me, I knew I had to reach out. That August I attended my first support group meeting.

Attending support group meetings quickly felt like shelter from a storm—a storm I found myself battling with my parents, my in-laws, my siblings, and non-homeschooling friends. My group provided a haven where I didn't have to explain our choice yet again. It was a place where like-minded moms and dads met to find information, friendship, and relief. I decided that I would never intentionally sequester myself and my children again.

Homeschooling is a mainstream choice now, and as a result more and more ways for homeschoolers to connect have developed. Some are strictly support groups, while others (such as co-ops or enrichment classes) endeavor to teach. Both exist to equip homeschool parents to provide a quality education and stand next to them as they stand up for their choice to teach their children at home. Participating in any such group is not only a "take" experience—it is a "giving" experience as well. What if you've graduated your children from homeschooling? If you have the gift of teaching or encouragement, you might consider offering those gifts to other people's children. The nature and needs of support groups is always changing to match the nature and needs of the homeschoolers they support. Find one that suits your family's needs right now.

Support Groups

There are as many different kinds of support groups as there are types of homeschoolers. Each differs in goals and style. They may also differ in the areas of size, the members of a family who are supported (just moms, dads, young children, teens, etc.), goals, frequency of meetings, requirements of members, how they're organized, and the cost to join. However, those differences aside, there are three major types of groups.

• *Religious.* The first place to check for a local support group is your home church. If they have a support group, consider joining at least so you can get to know the other homeschoolers in your church. Joining such a support group unites you with other Christian homeschoolers in a common faith. It provides fellowship in spiritual as well as practical areas of life. These groups will usually have a statement of faith that all members must either sign or agree to. The desire to be with like-minded homeschoolers is very strong. If you homeschool for religious reasons, you might experience confrontation in a secular group. We are called to encourage one another and to use our gifts to minister to one another. A faith-based support group helps accomplish both of these calls.

• *Secular.* There are just as many support groups that are not faith-based. They are open to everyone, regardless of beliefs. As you consider which groups to join, look to see if they have opportunities for yourself and your children to meet your family's needs. We were members of two different groups when we lived in Florida. Our state group was a secular group, but we also belonged to a small support group at our church. The larger secular group sponsored the state convention and regional support groups that offered field trips and enrichment classes.

• *Special-interest or special-needs.* More and more groups are forming as a result of a specific need or interest among homeschoolers. For example, gifted children who have been identified as such in the public schools are one of the fastest growing populations of homeschoolers. They form groups of their own for support because their needs are quite different than the average homeschooler. Other special-needs families have also formed their own support groups. Keep in mind that these families aren't isolating themselves from other homeschoolers. They are creating a support system that meets their needs, as we all should feel the freedom to do.

Support groups meet different needs at different times in our lives. As your child reaches the high school years, it is especially important to offer him or her opportunities to feel he or she is part of a group. Many support groups conduct formal graduation ceremonies. This is a way for the local homeschool community to come together in commencement—a celebration for what has been and a release for what is to come. Even small, church-affiliated groups can present the graduating homeschool seniors to the congregation for a graduation ceremony of some kind. This is a way to honor parents and to commission graduates.

CHOOSING A LOCAL SUPPORT GROUP

In an article included in the Christian Home Educators of Colorado's (CHEC) *Comprehensive Guide to Home Education*, author Terri Moon offers questions to ask to help you choose a local support group.

1. Is this group open to new members?
2. Is this group open to any home educator, or is it for families of a certain faith?
3. What are the goals of this group?
4. Is a certain age range of children the focus?
5. What activities are planned for the coming year?
6. Are dads involved, and if so, how?
7. What level of commitment is required of the members?
8. What is the cost of membership, both in money and volunteer time?

It's important to try to match your needs and expectations with what a group has to offer. Keep in mind that as your needs change, you might choose a different support group. Moon reminds us, "Don't choose a group only for what it can offer you, but for how it fits with the goals you have mapped out for your family and how you and your children can develop your gifts in serving others."

STARTING YOUR OWN SUPPORT GROUP

Sometimes the groups that already exist around us still do not meet our needs. You might be looking for something more intimate. Some groups are huge and have many activities going on, but you still need something more personal. You may run into other families who have not yet connected with a group and have the same vision for one. You may have a strong desire to serve other homeschoolers in your church by facilitating a support group. Whatever the reason, new support groups are forming all the time.

A new support group must be formed on a firm foundation. The following is a plan to get you started, adapted from points presented in Terri Moon's article listed previously.

1. Why is this group needed?
2. What goal(s) or needs would you like to meet?
3. Who will be the people involved?
4. When will you meet?
5. Where will you meet?
6. How will this group function?

AN INTERVIEW WITH PAM NEWBERG, HIGH COUNTRY HOME EDUCATORS SUPPORT GROUP LEADER

High Country Home Educators Support Group (in Colorado Springs) boasts more than five hundred families. From its humble beginnings, this group desired to meet the needs of homeschoolers first in their church and then in the larger community.

What is the importance of belonging to a homeschool support group?

Support groups can be especially beneficial to us as relational people. We need each other! Homeschooling is not always an easy road to follow. It takes sacrifice, hard work, time, commitment, energy, and the fruit of the Spirit. Most, if not all, moms (parents) will need support along the way. Like-minded people who are on a similar journey can offer lots of encouragement, fellowship, advice, direction, and just someone to listen.

Most homeschoolers encounter common struggles, and it's comforting to find out that you're not "the only one" who struggles in or with a particular area. I think of 2 Corinthians 1:3-4 in this situation: "Praise be to the God and Father of our Lord Jesus Christ, the Father of compassion and the God of all comfort, who comforts us in all our troubles, so that we can comfort those in any trouble with the comfort we ourselves have received from God." We really do have the capacity to spur each other on and to encourage each other in our homeschooling endeavors. Facilitating connection and fellowship for members is an important aspect of a support group.

What if you live in a remote area and there are no groups near you?

There are many options in this situation. One option would be to pray and ask God to show you who else is homeschooling in your area. You don't have to have a "formal" group to get support or do things together.

You can stay connected by using the phone or e-mail. Consider starting a small group if there are others interested. Some families think it is worth their time to drive in for meetings or field trips in order to get their support in surrounding areas. We frequently have had members drive from up to an hour away.

You can also subscribe to homeschool magazines or catalogs. The purpose of some of these is to offer encouragement and support through the mail. Online services are available to do this as well.

If you as a mother feel called to lead a support group, what should your considerations be?

The first thing to do is to get the approval of your husband. Pray together about this commitment. I think it is vital for you to have his support and approval before beginning. It is also important to count the cost of what this type of commitment would be. Do some homework, and find out what this may entail. Don't be a lone ranger—ask God for a partner or partners to work with. "Plans fail for lack of counsel, but with many advisers they succeed" (Proverbs 15:22). "Two are better than one, because they have a good return for their work: If one falls down, his friend can help him up" (Ecclesiastes 4:9-10).

It would be a great idea to pray and to form ideas, vision, and purpose together with others as a team. There is usually way too much to do alone; I think groups like this always have the potential to grow, and you should plan ahead for it. Also involve the husbands—they are incredible protectors (covering), sounding boards, and businessmen. They also balance us in so many ways.

Defining your group and its purpose and goals should be another consideration before you start. Make sure you have a plan before you begin. "Where there is no vision, the people perish" (Proverbs 29:18, KJV). It would also be good to talk with other group leaders or to read a good book about homeschool support groups to get ideas.

There are many things to consider as you pray and plan. Some of these things are: what type of leadership your group will have, how you will handle the finances, how you will handle volunteers, whether you will have membership requirements, how will you communicate to your members, and what services or functions you will provide.

When I was coming in as the group leader, I had many ideas from other groups about what our group should or could do. I had also read the "Support Groups of the Future" chapter in Michael Farris's book, *The Future of Homeschooling*. My vision was unrealistic, I believe, because I wanted to implement *all* these different things into our one group. Through prayer and counsel, God gave me this verse: "A discerning man keeps wisdom in view, but a fool's eyes wander to the ends of the earth" (Proverbs 17:24). I realized then that I needed God to show me what His purpose was for our group and that we needed to be prayerful, let the Lord direct our steps, and follow His lead.

What if the group you join doesn't meet your needs?

The first thing I would do is meet with the leadership and talk about my concerns. It may help the leadership to know what needs you have. All groups are different and meet different needs. Coming to an understanding about what the group is all about will help you in your decision to either participate or to find another group that will meet your needs better. God may also use this opportunity in a life-giving way to help enhance the group by either using your suggestions or your assistance.

Are there different types of groups?

There are many different types of support groups, and they can be defined in many ways. A support group can be defined by a religious affiliation, its size, the type of leadership it has, its membership requirements, location, purpose, means of communication, the different types of activities it has, and more. Some groups are for those using a specific curriculum or following a particular philosophy of homeschooling. Whatever type of group you have, it is important that each group is defined well, so prospective members can decide if this is the group for them or not, depending on their own needs. The things that define your group should be well publicized and communicated.

What have you personally gained as a support group leader? What have your children gained from this experience?

I believe I have gained a tremendous amount through these years as a support group leader. The biggest blessing is that I have had the opportunity to meet the most incredible ladies (and families). Homeschool moms are some of the most determined, selfless, courageous, and hardworking people I know. God has used these ladies and their families in my life to encourage, stretch, sharpen, love, and partner with my family and me as we homeschool together. I can't say enough what an incredible blessing it is to have met so many special people.

God has also used this opportunity to help me grow in areas of organization, administration, relational skills, juggling my priorities, and spiritually in areas of trusting Him, depending on Him, following Him, and so much more. I have so much more growing to do, but the Lord has certainly used this area of my life to do precious things.

As far as our children go, I do believe they have seen my husband and me in servant leadership roles, which I hope will be beneficial to them. They actually love to serve with us when they can.

CO-OPS

Co-ops, short for *cooperatives*, have increased in number exponentially over the past few years. Homeschooling is a mainstream phenomenon now, and with it comes many different people with many different needs. In the beginning it was understood that if you chose to homeschool, you were on your own. Now, however, families are reaching out to one another in support and instruction. When two or more families come together and agree to teach one another's children in at least one area, that is a co-op. Co-ops offer a break for the weary homeschool mom. Co-ops offer enrichment. Co-ops offer instruction in areas you may not feel equipped to teach, especially during the high school years. For some families, a co-op makes homeschooling all the way through high school a reality. Just as there are different kinds of support groups, there are different kinds of co-ops.

Parent Participation

Co-ops usually require at least some parent participation. For example, if four families form a co-op and they meet once a week, each teaching on a different enrichment topic, each parent would teach one out of every four weeks. That means they are off for three weeks out of every four. In co-ops that require more participation or are made up of more families, you may be asked to teach or volunteer in some other way every week. Very rarely will you find a co-op that does not require parent participation at all. It would then be classified as a school of some kind and not a co-op in the true sense of the term. Consider your level of participation carefully before committing to a co-op. Count the cost of your time honestly. Other families will count on you to honor any such commitment.

Does Size Matter?

Co-ops, like support groups, come in small, medium, and large sizes. Our family has participated in all three sizes at various points during our homeschooling experience. Just as in "Goldilocks and the Three Bears," you will have to find which size is "just right" for your family. A small co-op will be intimate and personal and will help you develop deeper relationships. But it may also require more of your energy, time, and resources. A medium co-op may offer more choices, more interaction, and less stress. But it may also cost more and be less personal and less flexible. A large co-op offers an almost endless variety of classes, offers students many different children to befriend, and usually is well organized. But it may also feel more like a school, cost more, and easily feel overcrowded and overwhelming to children and parents.

We participated in a very large co-op that offered many classes and gave our sons a taste of many topics. Later we participated in a medium co-op that operated more like a school. Our youngest son, Charles, preferred the medium co-op because he was with the same children all day long for the entire school year. It gave him a chance to form deeper friendships and feel a part of a community. However, our oldest son, Chris, preferred the larger co-op because experiencing many different topics was more important to him than relationships. As you get to know the needs of your children, you will make choices based on those needs. That may mean two (or more) different options.

AN INTERVIEW WITH LAJEAN HERTEL, ADMINISTRATOR OF HIGH COUNTRY ENRICHMENT CLASSES IN COLORADO SPRINGS, COLORADO

LaJean Hertel has her hands full serving the educational needs of more than seven hundred children in the enrichment classes offered through small-group ministries at New Life Church. This group is a model to anyone else developing co-ops or enrichment opportunities.

Can you tell us about the humble beginnings of High Country Enrichment Classes?

In 1996 we had two classes—Spanish and PE. At this time NLC was beginning "free market cells," which we now call "free market small groups." The idea is that people will come together for a common interest, and through that ministry can happen. When the idea of classes as cells was presented to the church, New Life thought that was a creative idea for using the church space (otherwise, renting a building would have been completely cost-prohibitive). So High Country Enrichment Classes was birthed under Small Group Ministry. We operate under the same principles, authority, etc. as any other New Life small group. We started with a handful of New Life families and in just six years are nearly four hundred families representing eighty-six churches (forty-one families with no church listed), and nearly seven hundred and fifty students. At that time High Country was managed by a board that incorporated in 1997. Later that board appointed three divisional boards—High Country Christian Academy (the umbrella school), High Country Support Group, and High Country Enrichment Classes. Each divisional board is overseen by the High Country Home Educators Corporate Board (which is comprised of two couples from each divisional board and any additional founding families). One key element in our ministry is having the men on the board, which has made an incredible difference in policy, in relationship issues, and in organizing our growing ministry. I became the Administrator in May 1998.

That summer we had an explosion of growth that we were unprepared for. Most of our classes closed, even after bumping up enrollment maximums. There was a sense of "this is what I've needed to be able to help my son/daughter or to continue to homeschool." Families I encountered at that time and since have been incredibly grateful for our classes, which caused them to feel empowered to homeschool their children. They didn't feel alone. Their children were connected, and they were connected in a positive and supportive, family-friendly environment. Originally the founding families thought we shouldn't be a co-op since we didn't want to require everyone to teach and at the time that was the only place to plug in. Instead we would pay our teachers (which would help families who could not afford to pay for classes—those who could not afford classes could teach). As we grew, more support positions became available for families who wished to receive credit for a portion of their classes. After a prayer and fasting time we believe God showed us that HCEC was merely a glove—that He was the hand to fill it and give it the ability to do anything.

Our ministry was to be fivefold in this priority order: the children, their families, raising leaders (through training and life coaching), "apostolic" ministry (to show others how to do what we do), and evangelistic ministry (praying that He would bring some who were unsaved and undiscipled, not to be a majority or we would have nothing to offer them, but that He would bring them). Operating under the NLC small-group ministry gave us a wonderful organizational model: The teacher is the small-group leader, and her class, the small group. The goal was ministry; the hook to get them in was whatever the class was about (in other words, they think they're taking debate, but they're really going to get discipled and ministered to as the Lord provides opportunities). Each teacher would be covered and supported by a section leader (who oversees four or five teachers). The section leaders answer to the Administrator, who is under the District Pastor. This model ensures better quality and accountability.

Everything we do is about facilitating the ministry that takes place in that classroom. We've had students ask for prayer for the most intimate family issues, seek counsel for the most serious teen issues, and be led to the Lord for the first time or again after a period away from Him. Families who have just moved to town have found a place to serve and connect. We have seen the whole Body of Christ work together to accomplish what one church alone could not do!

What are some of the reasons homeschoolers want enrichment classes?

The answers to this question are as numerous as the reasons why families choose to homeschool. In general, if a family feels weak in an area, enrichment classes can support them (which often enables them to continue their homeschool journey). Many of our families would not consider continuing to homeschool their high schooler without help in algebra, advanced math, biology, chemistry, or a foreign language. Families with younger children often feel weak in PE, art, or music and are strengthened by these supplemental classes. Families who are pulling a child from a school setting find it a good transition place where the child can connect with other children and still begin homeschooling. It doesn't feel like such a drastic change to the child. Many families simply want to be with other homeschooling families for fellowship and support, and enrichment classes are a good vehicle for that.

What are the characteristics of good co-ops? What are the characteristics of bad co-ops? What are some red flags?

I've addressed this in the question below as it seemed to flow that way.

Are there different types of co-ops?

There are probably many types of co-ops. In my experiences I have come across those that require participation from every family involved. Teachers are volunteers, and costs are usually minimal for administration and supplies. Then there is the exact opposite, like Grace Academy here in town, which is a drop-off "school" with paid teachers. The cost is reasonable, and there may be some ways for families to earn credit. Our ministry is unique to any I've seen. We pay our teachers, which opens the door for people from all walks (moms with young children, retired teachers, and some of our church employees with flexible schedules). We charge for classes but offer many opportunities for credit—teaching, Vital Partners (Teacher Assistants, Program Support: homework room, hall monitor, cleanup, etc., and Teachers' Tots—our childcare/preschool program for the children of those serving during a given hour). We also offer a financial assistance scholarship program.

I think whenever you "make" people participate in order to be a part, you potentially end up with poor placements—people in positions that don't fit their gifts or their season of life. For example, I would hate to require a mom who just started homeschooling or just had a baby to serve, teach, or even bake a cake just to have her children participate. That feels like a potentially heavy burden for one who may already be at her stress limit. It is so much better when participation comes from a burning desire to serve, teach, or bake a cake—from the heart—delight, not a duty. And that helps people last and not get burned out. The goal would be to present opportunities and match those with people's calls and gifts. That's a characteristic of a good co-op. A red flag would be when people are poorly placed. Their work will not be quality; they may be hurting or build resentment and may end up showing their frustration to the children or their families. This can create a domino effect of conflicts that will need to be managed. Complaining can also be a result of poor placement.

Another characteristic of a good co-op in my opinion is one that does its homework; in other words, its leaders screen and train those who teach and serve. It's a sad commentary on our society to have to do this, but it is the reality! We need to do applications, interviews, and even background checks on everyone who works with children. The Word says that a fool hires a passerby (Proverbs 26:10). We need to have systems for safety in place. I think the best co-ops have clear organizational procedures for handling conflict and evaluating staff and good accountability for finances. Open communication and accessibility to leaders and biblically grounded and operated co-ops are my personal preference.

A red flag for me is the lack of easy access to children. If parents are not allowed to drop in to visit a class, that is a red flag. Another red flag would be if there is no procedure in place for discipline, conflict, or grievances, for without such these things are handled arbitrarily. No accountability for finances would be another concern. One person (with no covering authority) being allowed to make all the decisions is usually a red flag as well.

One of the most important elements for a good co-op is to clearly articulate the ministry mission statement and to identify whom the co-op serves. Are the classes for strong Christians only or for anyone who is evangelical? Are they supplemental or core classes? Why do they exist, and who do they exist for? What are nonnegotiable requisites to participate? Often this is a living document, constantly growing and changing as the ministry grows and changes.

Are there different levels of parent involvement in co-ops?

Absolutely. And this may change as the organization changes. Some are or become drop-offs, some require parental participation with the children in the classes, and there is every possible scenario in between. If parents are paying for a service, they may expect to be less involved. If the co-op requires mandatory participation, parents may be involved physically but not with their heart. The ideal situation, of course, is participation and involvement by families because their heart is there—they can't not be involved!

Outline from your own experience steps to take to form your own co-op.

The first, obvious, step is to steep the undertaking in prayer. There are so many options and directions one could go that it is imperative to (as Henry Blackaby says in *Experiencing God*) find out where God is already working and join Him in His work (instead of our tendency to invite Him to join us in our work). Leaders should have several people interceding specifically for them.

Next, establish a decision-making, accountability group—either a board, an advisory committee, or a leadership team. It is important to articulate who has final authority for decisions, policy, and conflict resolution. Make clear who is accountable to whom and for what.

Determine the mission—why you exist, whom you exist for, and how you plan to accomplish this. This is the place to hammer out policy. Try to anticipate questions and scenarios that could arise, and prayerfully put in place a structure that will allow the focus to remain on the mission. We were so blessed to be under New Life Church, and much of our operation was determined by the way it operates. If your co-op is a ministry of a church, know that church's mission statement, hiring policies, honor code, etc. and operate similarly.

Invest in your leaders. Train them; equip them to serve well; make sure there is agenda harmony (that their personal reasons for participating fit well with your ministry's reason for choosing them). If your leadership is strong in service and can articulate the mission well, you are on your way with a strong foundation. If all of your leaders are developing leaders around them, your ministry will be deeply rooted and can then grow wide.

Offer your ministry to others; communicate clearly who you are so families can decide if it is a good fit for them. If God builds it, they will come.

There is much to be gained from either a support group or co-op experience. In fact, it is exciting to see how many different ways homeschoolers are getting together to help one another do this thing we call school. There is no reason to do it all alone. Support abounds! You can receive support, and you can offer it. Maybe joining a group isn't just for your benefit. Maybe you're there to encourage someone else who is close to burnout or is struggling with a difficult child or learning situation. Be willing to give at the same time that you are receiving.

But those who hope in the LORD will renew their strength. They will soar on wings like eagles; they will run and not grow weary, they will walk and not be faint.

—ISAIAH 40:31

RESOURCES

The Leaders' Manual: A Guide for Christian Home School Support Groups by Debbie Herron and Beth Hill (Christian Home Educators of Cincinnati, 4320 Tower Avenue, Cincinnati, OH 94127-1751). Covers subjects such as how to start a support group, leadership, co-op groups, children's activities, burnout, and city organizations.

8

CHILDREN WITH SPECIAL NEEDS

By Lindsey O'Connor

One of the greatest privileges I've had in my life has been the opportunity to homeschool my special-needs son. One of the greatest challenges I've had in my life has been the task of homeschooling my special-needs son. Let me tell you a little about both. When our family first began the journey into the special-needs world, no one realized that this challenging privilege would be the very thing God would use to hone our character, bless our family, and build up our son. All we knew at the beginning was frustration.

He was in the second grade at a Christian school, and he was struggling. I'd homeschooled him the year before and just couldn't understand why it was so difficult to teach him to read. After all, I'd taught his two older sisters, and they were great readers. We hoped the private school teachers would be the answer, but within weeks of the start of school the parent-teacher conferences and principal-parent conferences began. The part-time special education teacher began to pull him out of class several times a week and gave him his "special folder" of work to do in the classroom apart from what the other children were doing in order to modify his workload.

"We highly recommend testing him," they said. So we did. Two months later we sat at a large conference table with special education teachers and psychologists at the public school that had done the testing, and his problems were given a label. "Your son is learning disabled. He has dyslexia and central auditory processing disorder." My husband and I had a good news/bad news feeling. We were relieved that his difficulties were identified, for surely knowing the problem was the start to helping him; but at the same time we were shell-shocked. We now realized that he did not learn like most of the children in his class or like his siblings in our homeschool. Going by the teachers' report and our initial research, we believed expectations would have to be modified and methods changed, and he would be taught to compensate. We began to grieve—for his struggles, for the loss of high hopes for him, for his compromised future, and for the daily struggles of living and learning with a special-needs child.

In the midst of coming to terms with this emotionally, we began to cry out to the Lord for insight, wisdom, and direction. I also got busy researching. I went to the library and bookstore and began hours and hours of phone calls. I interviewed other moms of special-needs kids. I visited different specialists who offered various services. I began to understand that the world of learning disabilities couldn't be easily understood and that the approaches and viewpoints were many and varied.

I wanted a quick fix for my son. *We know what's wrong, so let's just fix it*, I thought. The Christian school and the public school were both very cooperative and agreed to work together to provide services for my son. After all, we now had an official IEP (Independent Education Plan) tailored for his needs, and he qualified for part-time special services through the school system that were free to me since his diagnosis brought federal funding to the school. The Christian school would continue pulling him out of class to work with him. While many families choose this kind of approach, I began to uncover information in my research that suggested this might not be the best solution for my son. Though that solution looked good on paper, it didn't address the emotional struggle he was enduring. And God began to direct my heart to the conclusion that the confusing conundrum of all the experts wasn't the route. God showed me and my husband that the path of help for our boy led home.

With a wave of apprehension, a great deal of blind faith, and a conviction that God was leading me, I began to homeschool my special-needs gift from God. If you are anywhere on this journey—realizing that your child learns differently, testing, grieving, researching, praying, accepting, or dealing with anger or discouragement—and you are considering homeschooling or wondering if you've made the right decision to home-educate your child, I want to encourage you. You can do it! The experts know a lot, and they are invaluable resources to us, but they are not the only ones qualified to educate a child with learning differences. There's one vitally important thing that they don't know—your child. You do. Better than anyone else. No one on the planet is more motivated to see your child excel and become all that God wants than you. And God, with His great omnipotence and unending wisdom, just waits to tenderly lead us as we educate our special kids and to help us learn what we need to help them learn.

Remember this—God did not make a mistake when He made your child, nor did He when He gave your child you for a mother. We live in a fallen world, but our children's conditions did not slip by Him. Seeing our children as the blessings they are begins with accepting them as they are, created by God for His purposes and His glory, not for ours or the world's, which has little room for merely average children or (gasp) under-average. This is not Lake Wobegon where all the women are beautiful and all the children are above average. This is kingdom living where we can look at our child and see him as God sees him—a blessing, regardless of his difference.

TYPES OF SPECIAL NEEDS AND APPROACHES

The differences our children face are vast, so I'll jump into the middle of the labeling controversy. Learning disabilities or differences? The medical and special education professions use labels to diagnose and differentiate our children. Many people, often parents, are opposed to labeling their children, fearing that will limit them and set a life course for them from which they will struggle to escape. Then there's the professional shift toward political correctness (pervasive developmental delay or mental retardation?); new names for common disabilities may avoid certain stigmas for the child but sometimes confuse the parents as to the real nature of the problem. Consider a balanced view. Labels, or more accurately appropriate testing results, can help us better understand what is going on neurologically and developmentally and where our child's greatest struggles lie, vital information for tailoring instruction for our child.

However, our child is not the label. We do not need the official definitions of learning disabilities that school districts use to qualify for state funding, but we should use the information to understand our child's strengths, weaknesses, and key learning difficulties so we can take action. Remember, however, that labels are not diagnostics leading to specific treatment. As Jerome Rosner says in *Helping Children Overcome Learning Difficulties* (New York: Walker & Company, 1993), "They are *descriptors of behavior* rather than identifiers of different conditions." Untold numbers of children are accomplishing far more than their "label" said they ever would. Yet don't avoid testing just to avoid the label—use the results to understand your child's learning struggles.

When living with special-needs children, more than one area is affected. Physical, emotional, developmental, behavioral, and social aspects can come into play. No wonder we sometimes feel overwhelmed.

There are also many types of special needs: medically fragile, mismatched children (child's learning style fighting with instruction method or environment), underachievers, learning disabilities, visual system disorders or visual perception disability, auditory system disorders, language processing disabilities, language/communication disorder, motor system disorders, attention disorders, slow learners, developmental disabilities (mental retardation), and autism. Wading through these problems and the vast methods and ideologies for addressing them can be daunting.

SCHOOLS OF THOUGHT FOR EVALUATING THERAPIES

One thing that was confusing to me in the beginning was the different schools of thought on methodology and the subsequent vast array of therapies available. I thought, *If we know a child has X learning disability, shouldn't the plan to help him be pretty straightforward? Can't we just take the test results and begin?* Not when we remember that a label is not a diagnosis with a set prescription for cure. To mix metaphors, it was more like walking into the biggest buffet known to man, dazzling choices set before me, and my choices wouldn't just be on my plate—they would be feeding my child for the future. I was overwhelmed with an overload of information and options. How do you choose when each therapy says its program can radically help your child and testimonials claim miracle cures and the school system says their IEP and their professionals are what your child needs? I discovered two things that helped: differentiating the schools of thought or approaches to treating learning problems, and realizing there is no one-stop shopping.

Compensation

This approach teaches to a child's strengths and helps the child go around his or her difficulties. For example, while modifying a child's workload, teachers might provide calculators for math, spell-checkers for language, and picture cards or cues for a child with a visual strength or cassette tapes for a child with auditory strengths. Many special education programs teach compensation techniques, especially with older children.

Remediation

These programs target the child's weaknesses and focus on improving his or her processing in those areas. Children might do exercises to strengthen short-term memory or listening therapies to strengthen auditory problems. These programs usually take some time to see results and can be expensive, but they can be quite effective. A homeschooling mom has an advantage in having the time and motivation to help strengthen her child's weaknesses.

Many feel that the best approach is to combine remediation and compensation methods.

Another ideological difference I discovered was in prognosis. When I left the big IEP conference where all the school professionals explained my son's test results and their plan for him, I was relieved to have answers, but I came away with the distinct impression that my son was facing a life-long problem. He would learn to read, and he would learn how to compensate, but he'd forever have these problems. But not everyone believes this. While learning disabilities don't just go away with instruction, like bacteria do because of antibiotics, I was encouraged to later find that there are differing opinions on prognosis. Some programs give more hope that certain learning problems can be corrected or greatly reduced instead of just worked around.

I also learned the important principle of a child's unlimited potential. Instead of viewing our child's problems through clinical definitions and therapy predictions alone, we need to remember that his or her potential needs to be unlimited by us. Certainly our child does have limits, but we do not really know where his or her limit is in any given area. Since we don't know where the line is exactly, and often the line of the capabilities changes, if we push and work as if our children have no limits we will often go much further with our children than we might otherwise. To me the idea of unlimited potential (balanced with realistic expectations of performance) offered greater hope than any other school of thought. It also leaves room for God to do more than we could ask or think.

The second thing that helped me out of therapy option overload after analyzing all the approaches was realizing that there is no such thing as one-stop shopping to help our children. There is no single therapy or program or diet or expert who is going to cure our child. When reading the claims of different therapies and the miracle testimonials, I wanted to find the solution that would fix my son. No one thing will "fix" our children. Instead I've learned that we need to choose what we think is best that is in line with how God is leading us, an agreeable methodology, what's affordable, and so on. I remember a woman at a Christmas party telling me one year about her program for her dyslexic son, and I got very enthused. She said, "You know, we've also changed his diet and his routine and do a number of other things with him in addition to this reading program, and frankly we may never know what is propelling him forward at any given moment." Instead of looking for "the fix," look at options of components in the plan (various therapies, diet, academics) to help your whole child.

CREATING A GAME PLAN

The information and tasks can seem overwhelming at first. When I first brought my son home from school, I remember thinking, *Where do I even begin?* Here are six broad steps to help you do just that.

Arm Yourself with Information

Read, research, and test your child. There are many excellent books, organizations, websites, and people who have walked this path before you that can help you gather information. Get recommendations in your area for where you can have your child tested. Consider public schools (it's free—we've paid for it with our tax dollars), private learning disability consultants, or universities. Testing can be arbitrary depending on the type given and your child's health that day, but good testing (which is often a series of tests over time) will help determine your child's weaknesses, strengths, and processing problems and should give information that will help you as you seek the program that's best for your child. The point of all this information is: Become an expert on your child and how he learns.

Consider Outside Help

A homeschool-friendly consultant may be the best investment you can make. Such persons can help interpret test results and directions you should take, and many can design an academic program tailored for your child. Or you may want to hire someone to look at the plans you've created and give advice. My son received excellent testing through the school, but I chose to decline their special education services. I took the results to a private consultant who added a test of her own, and I paid her to create his homeschool academic plan for the first year. Some outside therapies or programs include testing and/or academic planning or helps in their services like NACD and NILD (see the Resources section at the end of this chapter). The Homeschool Legal Defense Association has a special education specialist who can direct you to consultants in your area.

Choose Goals, Methods, and Curriculum

Your testing results, observations, and outside consultation can help you determine realistic goals for your child, both long-term (yearly) and short-term (the steps needed to reach long-term goals). Both yearly and short-term goals must be part of your plan for moving your child forward in each academic area and in relation to his or her specific academic and developmental struggle. Choose your methods for reaching those goals. Just be sure that your methods are *structured* and *systematic*, two vital ingredients for a special-needs program. Will you incorporate remediation, compensation, or a combination of techniques? Will your program be multisensory? In what subjects? Will you use textbooks or a literature-based, "real-book" approach? If you are new to homeschooling, read about the different approaches to homeschooling (classical, unit study, traditional, Charlotte Mason, etc.), and choose what fits the way your child learns, then tailor it for his or her special needs. However, the "unschooling" approach is highly discouraged for most special-needs children because it lacks two things they greatly need—structure and a systematic approach. Many moms like to combine methods to produce an eclectic, customized program. For example, you might want to use a scaled-back classical program with traditional textbooks for a few subjects while incorporating your favorite Charlotte Mason ideas such as narration, short lessons, nature study, and living books.

After choosing your methods, choose your curriculum to accomplish that method. You can purchase materials through suppliers' catalogs, online, or at homeschool conventions or specialized or children's bookstores with homeschool sections. The book *Homeschooling Your Special Needs Child* lists and comments on various curricula that work well for special-needs kids.

Write Your Own Individualized Education Plan

This doesn't have to look like an IEP prepared for a child receiving special education services in school, and there is no set form. It is simply a written plan tailored to your child's specific learning differences and weaknesses for that year. Include the following: your child's present ability (grade levels reached in each academic area and developmental levels), your goals, methods, and curriculum (discussed above), and a progress notes or evaluation section where you can periodically record how your child is doing in each area. Creating your own IEP (or having a consultant help you with one) is important. It provides documentation for you and for any outside party who may question your right to home-educate a special-needs child, it keeps you moving toward your goals, and it allows you to document your child's progress.

Organize for Success

This is important for any project, but it's critical here. Our special kids usually have trouble organizing themselves, so we must help them. We also need to organize ourselves, so we are prepared for a smoothly running program. I've found it helpful to organize my child *and* myself in three areas—*structure, schedule, materials*. All children are served well with structure in their lives, but special learners *must* have it. They need to know that their day is not just one long string of random events over which they have no control. When we provide routines and blocks of time and activities that they can anticipate, we remove some uncertainty and frustration for our children and create the framework for ourselves for implementing our program. Both mom and child have less stress.

Think of your structure as the foundation and steel girders and your schedule as your builder's approach to completing the project. Structure could include set rising and bed times, two meals together at home at regular times, a chunk of time for academics, a block of time for play, another for chores, and other things that are important for you and your child to accomplish daily that your child can expect. Your schedule is your unique plan to make that happen. If you are a scheduled person by nature, you'll wonder why others struggle in this area. If you are a spontaneity-loving mom, you may need more help to be able to organize your child's time. It's helpful to separate the ideas of structure and schedule. We must have the structure (think blocks and priorities), while the schedule can vary among families, children, or seasons of life. If one doesn't work, try something else. Tweak it, then stick with it for consistency and habit development. I was stressed and miserable under the burden of trying to implement *someone else's* idea of what my schedule should look like, until I figured out what worked best for me and my son. Another tip that helped me tremendously was to schedule more time than each thing takes. Then we have wiggle room on bad days and can push forward on good ones.

Organizing our materials is the last step to organizing for success. (Vicki Caruana's book *The Organized Homeschooler* is great for this.) Special-needs children often can't wait while we scrounge for missing items. Set up a place for files, bookshelves, reference materials, grab-and-go, easily accessible storage for the items we use daily with our kids, containers for art supplies, paper, pencils, etc., and an extra stash for you to which your children don't have access. Set up your children with a notebook that contains paper, folders, their schedule, their daily assignment plan, a place to record things they must remember, and a zippered pouch with two pencils (always) and their other supplies. Teach them how to keep it all in good order (file, don't stuff; always replace lost pencils, etc.) by checking it daily for three weeks, then periodically. I supplied my kids with a bin with a carrying handle to hold all their books (portable school when needed) and taped an end-of-school checklist to the lid listing what they needed to do to be prepared for the next day. I remember watching a learning therapist with my son some years ago. She accomplished so much in so little time! Then I noticed that everything she needed was where it was supposed to be and right at her fingertips. She was efficiency in motion because her materials were so well organized. Habits, regular maintenance, and training our children where to put things help us from losing them to never-never land when they have to get up to search for that lost pencil.

Secure the Safety Net

This is our prayer support, a plan for rough days, ongoing testing, and accountability. We've chosen an incredibly rewarding but challenging path, so we need support in a big way. Let your family and close friends know how you are doing regularly. The dailyness of a special-needs child can wear us down emotionally and physically. We need a support network that will listen, pray for us and our child, and even help when the path gets rocky. We also need a backup plan for when we or our child are having a tough day. If children are resistant, we need to stick to our guns; but if they are "off" that day or are frustrated, we need an alternate plan that accommodates them without leaving us feeling like we aren't accomplishing our goals. For example, do half of the math problems, or have them dictate to you instead of writing, or have an alternate schedule for hard days. It also helps to provide repeat testing for our child to track the progress of our program and to look for someone who can help provide some accountability and feedback for us. It may be an outside organization, another mother of a special-needs child, or our spouse.

The greatest safety net of all is the arms of our heavenly Father. On days when I waver between wanting to send my child to a Tibetan boarding school and weeping for his needs, days when I feel like he'd be better off with anyone other than me, I find comfort in knowing that God loves me and my child more than I can imagine and that He did not make a mistake in our family. His Word is a comforting quilt on such days.

THE TOP TEN THINGS WE CAN DO WHILE HOMESCHOOLING OUR SPECIAL KIDS

These are my top recommendations for helping a special-needs child, culled from many sources over the years including the school of experience. They are good for all kids, but vital for special needs.

Create a Positive Environment

For every one negative comment or action, try to see that the child has four or more positive ones. Keep a data sheet several times a day for a week and you might be surprised. The four to one ratio can motivate struggling children and create a safe place for them to be who God made them.

Be Consistent

Small steps done consistently get our children much farther than huge leaps and stops.

Have Clear Expectations, Rewards, and Consequences

Write down rules. Make lists for the child of what you want him or her to accomplish. Pick one or two problems to focus on at a time, and give lots of opportunities to implement consequences for violations and reward or respond positively (with intensity) for the things he or she does right.

Give Lots of Input

Provide lots of input, and require modified output at the right frequency, intensity, and duration. Give information to the child in a multisensory fashion with the repetition he or she needs. Modify the output (writing, tests, recitation, etc.) to his or her capability. A school classroom's ratio of input to output is much different than a special-needs homeschool's ratio. Our kids learn better when information is presented with high frequency (as often as they need to get it and retain it), great intensity, and short duration.

Give the Child Opportunities for Surefire Success

School can feel like failure to a struggler; so we must help our special-needs children find things that they can do well and modify other requirements so they experience success.

Create Structure

It's the backbone of their day.

Praise, Praise, Praise Them!

Only prayer is more powerful.

Limit Overstimulation

Create a language-rich environment with books and audio to counter our visual culture. Limit electronics, video, and noise, and do all possible for a serene learning and living environment.

Provide Good Nutrition

Don't panic over the immense diet and the possibilities for supplements; just begin by increasing good foods while decreasing bad ones. Add lots of green veggies (phytonutrients) and a daily multi-vitamin, and limit the sugar, preservatives, colorings, junk/fast food, and allergens. Then look into supplements if you feel led.

Think "Unlimited Potential"

No one really knows the exact limit of a child's capability, although some well-meaning folks have tried to tell us otherwise. When we shift gears from looking at children's limitations to looking at their potential, we will take them farther.

KEEPING MOMENTUM HIGH AND BURNOUT AT BAY

Living with and teaching a special-needs child can be incredibly trying. So the following precautions can combat burnout and keep us moving forward as parents while we continue to move our children forward. We can:

• Continue to stay connected with what inspires us (books, conferences, tapes, support groups, e-mail loops, digests, discussion groups, other parents).

• Ask God to renew our convictions and to reveal spiritual fruit in ourselves and in our children. Sometimes that is the one thing that keeps me going.

• Keep written records of successes and progress (academic, frustration tolerance, organization, cooperation, behavior, spiritual growth, emotions, language). We can review this, especially when we feel like we're not getting where we'd like.

• Evaluate our child against how far he's come, not against other children. Look at grade level skills lists and state requirements to help when writing our yearly IEP's, so we have high enough expectations; then modify them for our child. We should not look at these lists or our friends' children and compare.

• Think creatively during tough times. Consider new methods or a new schedule. Ask God, the author of creativity, to reveal what our children need. I even had to expand my thinking about my child's future from a college-of-course mind-set to the wide possibilities that God might have in store instead.

• Keep praying. This is our source of strength, power, hope, and change, and it changes us.

• Renew ourselves. A mother who gives until she is depleted cannot serve her child. Find the things that fill our cup and make them a part of our life. The whole family wins.

• Keep family needs in balance. The good of the whole family must be balanced with the needs of its individuals. We stopped one very effective outside therapy a few years ago because the cost for the whole family was too great. And maintain your marriage at all costs!

• Keep having fun! What do we love to do? What thrills our children? What small joys can we add to our day?

• Strive for a balanced, enriched life. Academic gains at all costs is no way to live, special needs or otherwise. God cares about our whole person—body, soul, and spirit—not just our minds.

Why It's Worth the High Cost

Anything worth anything is expensive; so we must consider the cost to value ratio. What does this cost, and is it worth it? Here's a short but frank look at the cost of home-educating a special-needs child. It takes energy, money, and time. Lots of energy and time. It can be emotionally draining. It demands a high level of commitment. It requires great consistency. It can be personally limiting. We will not have the carefree life of a mother who puts her child on the school bus and makes luncheon dates, nail appointments, or career or hobby plans anytime she wishes. Ultimately, it requires self-sacrifice.

So why is it worth it? Why would we choose to do this? Here are a few reasons.

It offers large amounts of one-on-one tutoring in a loving, positive environment, which is the optimum for learning. A special-needs specialist recently told me she was trained at an expensive school for learning-disabled boys. The headmaster had a large staff and required that every boy receive at least one hour a day of individual tutoring. "We can't help these kids like they need if we don't provide this," he said. A similar school in my area charges about fifteen thousand dollars a year. Even with that price tag, they don't come close to the amount of individual tutoring that I can give my son at home. A teacher friend of mine said, "I went into special education because I truly believed I could make a difference and help. With over twenty kids in my class I couldn't, and it breaks my heart." In the home environment we are able to sculpt a tailored, individualized, changeable program.

It's also worthwhile to avoid some of the problems of the special education track in a public school including labeling, cruelty from other kids (who figure out who's different regardless of the way the program is structured), self-esteem issues for our child, and lowered expectations. Children need realistic but high expectations, and we can offer that.

It's worth it to decrease the anger, resentment, low self-worth, and plummeting motivation driven by an academic failure cycle. We can instead increase our child's view of himself as a capable and unique child of God.

Homeschooling a special-needs child is family-centered, not expert-centered. I'm grateful for outside help, but once I realized I could do this, that I was an expert on my child, the family regained center. We can utilize outside help, but my child is not dependent on the village.

Any price is worth helping our child reach his or her potential and become the young man or woman God wants. An added and unexpected perk is that *we* are changed in the process. God puts families together for His purposes. I used to say, "I'm the wrong mom for what my child needs." Not anymore. Working with my child flings my weaknesses out into the spotlight, forcing me to change, strive toward things I might not have otherwise, and lean daily on God for strength I don't have on my own. This process, part of His plan, is slowly chiseling me more into the image of Christ. I'm learning patience when I think I have none left, how difficult and beautiful unconditional love is, that this spontaneous right-brainer mom can learn structure, consistency, and discipline through teaching my son.

God's timing always amazes me. After I started writing this chapter, I hit a wall in my own homeschool. For many reasons I began zealously looking for other educational options. I left no stone unturned. I visited principals and classrooms, investigated department philosophies and methodologies, interviewed and took copious notes. I looked at lots of school options: charter, public, Christian, a learning disabilities school, and even a cottage school in someone's home. My ultimate conclusion? What I wrote above. My flesh wanted another choice, but God led me back to the convictions that led me to begin this journey in the first place. And I am at peace being convinced of the things I have written to you and confident that God has led us and will enable us. There is great joy in the fruit of such a choice, in seeing the child you cherish flourish, and there's also incredible joy in obediently following where God leads.

Lindsey O'Connor began homeschooling her children in 1989. She and her husband, Tim, have five children from college to the cradle. Lindsey's firsthand experience homeschooling a special-needs child is an encouragement to us all. Lindsey, a former broadcaster, is also a speaker and the author of If Mama Ain't Happy, Ain't Nobody Happy *(Harvest House, 1997) and other books.*

RESOURCES
Books
Learning in Spite of Labels by Joyce Herzog (Greenleaf Press, 1994).
Homeschooling Children with Special Needs by Sharon C. Hensley (Noble Publishing, 1995).

Organizations

National Academy of Child Development (NACD)

P.O. Box 380
Hunstville, UT 84317-0380
801-621-8606
www.nacd.org — e-mail: info@nacd.org

NACD designs family-centered, home-based, neuro-developmental programs for all levels of special needs children.

NATHHAN (National Challenged Homeschoolers Associated Network)

Christian Families Homeschooling Special Needs, Disabled Children and Adoption
P.O. Box 39
Porthill, ID 83853
208-267-6246
www.nathhan.com — e-mail: nathanews@aol.com
Their website is a must-visit!

National Institute for Learning Disabilities (NILD)

107 Seekel St.
Norfolk, VA 23505-4415
757-423-8646
www.nild.net — email: info@mail.nild.net

NILD provides an individualized program of educational therapy with trained educators designed to stimulate cognitive and perceptual functioning.

Homeschool Legal Defense Association (HSLDA)

P.O. Box 3000
Purcellville, VA 20134-9000
540-338-5600 — e-mail: info@hslda.org

HSLDA provides legal covering and has a special-needs coordinator.

Other websites regarding special needs:

LD Online — www.ldonline.org

Learning Disabilities Association of America — www.ldanatl.org

Recordings for the Blind and Dyslexic — www.rfbd.org

National Information Center for Children & Youth with Disabilities (NICHCY)
www.nichcy.org

9

STUDY SKILLS

I looked at the sea of faces of fourth through sixth grade homeschoolers, looking back at me wide-eyed and utterly confused. I agree that learning Latin word roots can be intimidating if you are unfamiliar with it, but the task of learning ten roots per week should not be overwhelming. This was the second week of class, and the results of their first homework assignment were dismal at best. Half of the students did not even remember to do the homework. The other half did not complete it, or did it incorrectly. Upon investigation, I realized many of my students did not know how to use a dictionary, set time aside for homework, or memorize for testing purposes. Even though this was an enrichment class, I decided that those skills were necessary, not only to experience success in this Latin word roots class, but in future educational experiences. I decided it was necessary to spend a couple of weeks teaching them those skills.

Being at home you don't have homework. Being at home you don't have to figure things out on your own. Being at home can sometimes leave holes in learning. We don't know what is in our children's futures, but we should take some time to prepare them for an educational career away from home someday. Parents have told me, "He's not going to college; he'll run the family business. He won't need study skills." This breaks my heart for two reasons. One, shouldn't children decide for themselves what they want to be when they grow up? Two, study skills encompass more than memorization of facts. The self-management components are valuable skills for anyone in any profession. Whether your child is college-bound or bound to take *any* kind of class outside of home, he needs to fine-tune his study skills.

Learning how to learn is a cognitive skill that utilizes strategies that encourage success. There are tools or strategies that are cognitive, physical, and motivational. These categories roughly match mind, body, and spirit. All require forming new habits and in many cases breaking old ones. Our time is so precious. It's important that we learn to redeem it. Learning or study skills can help our children redeem their time and become better stewards of the time they have.

MIND SKILLS

Cognitive skills are thinking skills. One of the first steps to sharpening the cognitive skills listed below is *self-reflection*. Our children need to become comfortable reflecting on how they are doing. They need to be able to assess both their strengths and their weaknesses. They need to choose areas in which they can improve and thoughtfully consider how to move from competence to quality. Whether they are at home or in a school, they must learn how to consider the job they're doing and how well they're doing it.

Once self-reflection is a habit, the following mind skills will lead them to successful learning experiences.

Listening

Believe it or not, we spend more time listening than reading, speaking, or even writing. However, there is a difference between active and passive listening. In order for children to learn, they must be active listeners. When you're an active listener, you "make the effort to comprehend, appreciate and evaluate the speaker's message" (A. D. Wolvin and C. G. Coakley, *Listening Instruction*, Urbana, IL: ERIC Clearinghouse on Reading and Communication Skills, 1979). If your child finds himself or herself in a classroom situation, listening will be the main task. Sometimes our children hear us, but they're not listening. That's why exasperated parents everywhere cry, "Are you listening to me?"

We can encourage active listening in non-school-related activities first by holding our children accountable for their listening. We want to make sure 1) that they actually heard us, and 2) that they can tell us what we said. Comprehension can only happen with these two prerequisites. Active listening is respectful listening. Expect your children to answer you with "Yes, Mom" or "Yes, Dad." It is a sign of respect, but it is also an indicator that they heard you.

When I taught in the public schools, I had to build good listening behavior into my students. Somehow they came to school without it! Even for middle schoolers, I'd ask, "What makes a good listener?" The correct answer is: eyes on the speaker, mouth closed, and hands still. Everyone who speaks believes they have something of value to say. They desire to be listened to. No one wants to be ignored. Becoming an active listener not only fosters successful learning, it fosters successful and satisfying relationships.

Sometimes the greatest struggle we have in our marriages is being listened to. "He doesn't listen to me," "She always has to have the last word," and "In one ear, out the other" are common marital gripes. Maybe we can raise our children to be better listeners than we ourselves have been. Maybe it's not too late for us to learn to be active listeners as well.

Participation

Remember when *class participation* was part of your grade? That was always a hard one for me. I was quiet and shy, and inevitably that space on my report card always read, "Needs improvement." I was an active listener, but not an active participant. Even as homeschoolers, we need to encourage our children to participate in the learning process. If you use a prepared curriculum (textbooks, workbooks, etc.) only, it is more difficult for your child to actively participate. There's nothing for him to do but go through the material in a rote manner. If you use a unit study for at least part of your homeschooling, your child will naturally participate, because that is the nature of a unit study. Being an active participant means applying the information learned.

Your child may find himself in a traditional classroom at some point, either in an enrichment class or a public school classroom on a part-time basis. Either way, teachers expect students to participate in five kinds of activities. The following activities are adapted from those presented by Gall, Gall, Jacobsen, and Bullock in their book *Tools for Learning* (Alexandria, VA: ASCD, 1990).

1. *Answering the teacher's questions.* Question and answer time is usually part of every school day. Teachers use this time as an opportunity to rehearse, interpret, and apply what students know. Find your own opportunities at home to ask your children questions about what they are learning and what you are teaching. There are different types of questions, and it is important to vary your use of the different types. *Literal* questions are fact-based (what?). *Interpretive* questions cause students to make inferences about what they've learned (why?). *Applied* questions cause students to use the information they've learned (how?).

2. *Seat-work.* Teachers assign seat-work to give students time to practice skills and to process new information on their own. This is a good time for students to find out what they've learned, and if they don't understand a concept, this is also a good time to ask questions. Some homeschoolers do an inordinate amount of seat-work, especially those who almost exclusively use workbooks. Seat-work should happen, ideally, after instruction, in order for it to be effective. It should not be used in lieu of instruction.

3. *Inquiry.* We can use inquiry to evaluate how a child processes the

information he has been presented during instruction. Inquiry is frequently used in the sciences, but it is also quite an effective tool to use in language arts and literature studies. In order for inquiry to be profitable for students, they must learn how to "observe objects or events, detect patterns, and make inferences from them" (Gall, Gall, Jacobsen, and Bullock). Students must learn to draw their own conclusions about what they've learned. Inquiry is a means to that end.

4. *Small-group discussions.* These discussions can be used to evaluate students' comprehension and inquiry skills. Students learn to think and express themselves, exchange ideas, and work cooperatively. There are rules to small-group discussions, and students must learn to adhere to those as well. Even with my own two boys, we would have a "small group" discussion about a story we read together. Why did the character do what he did? Was it worth it? Could he have handled his problem differently? A family is a small group. Use it to help your children practice these skills.

5. *Student presentations.* Student presentations help students improve their thinking, speaking, and cooperative work skills. Even though presentations cause anxiety in many students, the more often they do them, the more at ease they will become with the process. The key is to start young. Student presentations involve more participation than any other activity presented here. They give students complete control of the learning process for those moments they are on center stage. Even as homeschoolers, we can offer our children opportunities to take center stage. You can do this within your family at the end of a particularly interesting unit study. If you join a 4-H club in your area, your child will be required to make presentations. When you present information, you are in a sense the teacher. It is a well-known fact that if you are able to teach the concept or material to someone else, you have really mastered it yourself.

Taking Notes

Taking notes is what I would consider a necessary evil. Whether or not your child has good penmanship doesn't matter. What matters is whether he or she can listen to the information presented and write it down in an efficient and comprehendible manner. He will use these notes to study from later. An integral skill to note-taking is the ability to distinguish pertinent information from irrelevant information without the teacher saying, "This is important. Write it down!" We can practice this skill with our children when they watch a video related to what they are studying or to a field trip. Make sure they have pen and paper in hand so they can jot down all relevant information. They can then use that information to create either a report or some other individual project. You can use their report or project to evaluate whether or not they learned the information required.

If, later in life, they find themselves in a classroom setting, they will be more comfortable with note-taking. Good note-taking is a valuable skill. Remember when you were absent from school and needed the notes from a particular class? You always turned to someone you knew took good notes. When your children go to college, not only will note-taking be a survival skill, they will use it when they read textbooks on their own and decide for themselves what is relevant and what isn't.

Memorization

From my own experience, it always seemed as if there were kids who were good at memorizing and those who weren't. I wasn't. I did exceptionally well in math until geometry, where I had to memorize theorems and such. Studying for a vocabulary test was excruciatingly difficult for me. Why did it seem that some kids could memorize and I couldn't? Even now, memorizing a Bible verse is a challenge for me. However, both of my children have exceptional memories. They don't have to work very hard to remember anything.

Memory work is required for much of what we learn. How else can a child learn his math facts except by memorizing them? The idea is to move information from short-term memory storage to long-term storage. It has to become a part of you in such a way that retrieving and using that stored information is both effortless and habitual. It took longer than expected, but my youngest son, Charles, now knows his times tables "cold." As he ventures into division, he can retrieve the necessary facts without struggle or hesitation.

In her book *How to Parent So Children Will Learn* (New York: Three Rivers Press, 1996), author Sylvia Rimm explains that in order "to move material from short-term memory to long-term memory, you have to (1) make it meaningful, (2) organize it, and (3) rehearse or practice it. All these strategies will cause that information, boring or otherwise, to move to long-term memory for retrieval."

Organization

We run a pretty organized household, but personalities can always mess up the system. Our oldest son is quite gifted intellectually; however, he leans toward being organizationally impaired! He sometimes reminds us of the absent-minded professor. More than once he will tell us he cannot find something only to have either his father or I walk right into his room and pick it up. When we homeschooled him, the consequences of disorganization weren't as dire. But he went back into school in sixth grade—middle school—which can be an organizational nightmare for even the most structured and regimented student. Keeping track of seven classes with seven different teachers and seven different requirements can quickly become overwhelming. It is definitely a survival skill in the grades between six and twelve. Even if you homeschool your children all the way through high school, they must acquire organizational skills. College shouldn't be the first time they are on their own to manage their classes.

BODY SKILLS

Study and practice are not strictly mind matters. There are physical considerations as well. For example, I know I can't study effectively in my own bedroom. It's too comfortable—the bed is too inviting! I also know myself well enough to know that I need complete quiet when I study (although there was a time in my teens when I studied with music playing in the background). I also know that I am a night person. I do my best work and retain more after 6 P.M. All of these figure into successful study habits. Do you know your child well enough to know how, when, and where he or she studies best?

A Time and Place

Setting a regular time and place for study is crucial for a productive study session. When you sit in the same place for daily studying, your automatic responses will be conditioned to concentrate when you assume your study position. It is the forming of a new and productive habit that caters to successful studying. This is not unlike what sleep experts say about sleep: Go to bed at the same time every night; use the bed for sleep only (not television watching, toys, studying or eating, etc.). That way, when you go to your bed at night, your body knows it's going to sleep.

Some children already accomplish their work independently and study in a timely manner, so there's no need for you to set a time and place for them. But others do not work long enough, and you should structure their time and place for them. Keep in mind your child's learning preferences. Some are distracted by noise; others are distracted by quiet. Our youngest does better if he does his work in the middle of things, with others around him. Our oldest son needs peace and quiet. Take these needs into account.

Some basic tips to setting up productive study times and places are: Use a timer to enforce how long your children work, insist on no television (or computer or video games or even reading for pleasure) until work or study is complete, and provide breaks when they begin to tire. If your child is enrolled in some sort of enrichment class or other class outside the home, he will need time to complete his assignments or to study for a test. Encourage him to complete this work prior to dinner. Often if study time is set late in the evening, students have difficulty concentrating, and studying is not likely to be efficient.

Study for Visual Learners

Visual learners can see information in their minds. They can remember spelling words and other information after studying them for only a few minutes. They pay attention to details, and their work is generally neater than those who are stronger either as an auditory or kinesthetic learner. In her book *21 Days to Helping Your Child Learn* (Grand Rapids, MI: Zondervan, 1998), author Cheri Fuller calls the visual learn a *looker*. She outlines strategies for each kind of learner, and I've adapted them below. Regarding the visual learner:

1. *Make an illustrated time line* if dates need to be learned. Use graphics and other illustrations to help your child remember what he or she learned.

2. *Make study cards* using colored index cards to help your child memorize things for most any subject.

3. *Utilize color* to categorize information. Use a different color highlighting pen for different concepts.

Study for Kinesthetic Learners

Kinesthetic learners try to do everything by doing and touching. They tend to get fidgety if they have to sit for long periods of time. Pencil and paper assignments bore them. Try to provide hands-on experiences for as many different topics as you teach. According to Cheri Fuller, these are great study strategies for *movers*:

1. *Facilitate concrete (hands-on) experiences* like experiments, field trips, and role-playing to make the learning more mover-friendly.

2. *Get a black or white board*, and have your child teach the concepts to younger siblings.

3. *Help your child create a board game* of his own design to show what he or she has learned; then play it.

4. *Use demonstration whenever possible*. Then have your child demonstrate the concept or skill back to you or to younger siblings.

Study for Auditory Learners

Auditory learners are highly verbal and are good at listening and following oral directions. They like to work with others and easily express their feelings and ideas. According to Cheri Fuller, *talkers* work as if "they have high-quality tape recorders in their brains." Here are some talker study strategies:

1. *Make information to be learned into a poem or rhyme or song.*

2. *Practice dictation skills* with your child. Read aloud a passage (length determined by age and experience), and have your child write the passage on a piece of paper. Work through his spelling and grammar skills this way.

3. *Allow your child to study with someone else.* They can discuss the material and then choose questions for a practice test they can take and score.

Learning styles are gateways to success for your child. Help him or her to study through his or her strengths and he or she will be more efficient.

Spirit Skills

Educational literature is full of articles and research about how to motivate students. Some of these ideas are appropriate for our children as they wrestle with how best to study. Being a successful student takes more than addressing how the mind works and what the body needs. We always need to address the needs of the soul or the spirit as well.

Reward Yourself

I remember pulling all-nighters preparing for exams in college. Some kind of chocolate was my reward for studying for two hours straight. Between that and coffee, the night would fly by! Obviously, you don't have to dangle food in front of your child to get him to spend time studying. However, some kind of reward helps break up the time, especially if your child is a *mover* (kinesthetic learner). Let your child decide what he should reward himself with. My oldest son, Christopher, loves to read. His reward for himself is usually half an hour of reading. My youngest son, Charles, prefers to go outside and play as a reward. Even now, as a full-time writer, I reward myself for every two hours of writing.

Value-driven

Our children need to know that we value the time and effort it takes to study. We value persistence when the task is long or difficult. We value a job well done. Just because you homeschool your children doesn't mean they truly understand your passion to provide them with a quality education. What's important to you will become important to them. Talk about it. Make decisions based upon those values. Point out good study habits when you see them in your child. Congratulate him or her on a job well done.

Independence and Privacy

We have to be careful as homeschoolers that our children have time on their own to complete their studies. By the fourth grade most children are capable of working independently on most of their studies. If you are certain that they understand the task and you have taken the time to instruct them on new material, step away and expect them to complete their work on their own. If they have difficulty, encourage them to review the material at least three times before they ask for help. Don't sit with them the entire time they are working (unless you have a child who is more than easily distracted). If you do need to help them when they are confused, then be sure they go back and complete the assignment on their own.

If your child is enrolled in an enrichment class or some other traditional class, he will have homework or special projects that he or she is expected to complete on his or her own. You should work with him or her on any special projects, especially if this is a new task to him or her, but make sure you are just a guide and don't become heavily involved.

When graded work comes home from that traditional class, show interest, but don't impose. Be involved in the completion of the work to make sure he or she is following the teacher's directions and is turning in the work on time. But don't take on the teacher's role in this case. Our children need to learn to adhere to another teacher's expectations at this point.

Do you have time to teach study skills? Can you afford not to? There will come a time, sometimes sooner than later, when our children will be in someone else's classroom besides our own. For some, that first time away may not be until college. There are many homeschool success stories regarding college acceptance and performance, but there are many other stories of disappointment, discouragement, and disaster. Start early on the road to success by providing your children with the tools of learning. Good study and work habits can master the most challenging classes or teachers.

RESOURCES

How to Parent So Children Will Learn by Sylvia Rimm (Three Rivers Press, 1996).
Tools for Learning: A Guide to Teaching Study Skills by M. D. Gall, Joyce P. Gall, Dennis R. Jacobsen, and Terry L. Bullock (ASCD, 1990).
21 Days to Helping Your Child Learn by Cheri Fuller (Zondervan, 1998).
How to Be School Smart: Super Study Skills by Elizabeth James and Carol Barkin (Beach Tree, 1998).

10

MUSIC EDUCATION

By Laurinda Curti

From birth to age six, I lived in a ranch home in a suburb of Cleveland, Ohio. My father built the first underground swimming pool in the city in our backyard. My parents put me in that pool as an infant. They splashed water on me and gently lifted me in and out of the water. During the summers we were in that pool all the time. I remember as a toddler teaching myself to paddle and kick in the water. My younger sister and I would play with various water toys in and around the edges of the pool for hours. We literally had no fear of this huge skill called swimming and performed various techniques according to our abilities.

Then during the summer of my sixth year my parents moved to the other end of town. There was no pool around anywhere. What once was becoming second nature to me was now a lost skill. All my confidence in swimming disappeared. To this day my swimming skills are elementary at best. So when my four children came along, it was not an option—they began swimming lessons by age three.

My first daughter, Andrea, screamed, kicked, cried, and resisted the thought of going in the pool. Nonetheless, I told the instructor to take her out of my arms, put her in the pool, and do what she could with her. Sure enough, by the end of the first week she settled down, gained confidence in her teacher, and began to learn to swim. We have four children, with varying natural abilities toward swimming. Each ultimately learned to swim because of opportunity, practice, and encouragement.

Teaching music to children is a lot like teaching them to swim. Along with developing a deep appreciation of the spiritual aspects of God's creation, the goals are to provide an enjoyable and fun experience, to provide the foundation for a lifelong skill that will have many applications, and to assist in building a strong, positive self-image. In order to accomplish these goals, training needs to begin as early as possible, along with constant and consistent exposure to various musical experiences. In addition, a child's learning style, desires, and goals, along with his or her parents' goals, should be analyzed and evaluated so the appropriate teaching environment can be chosen to meet those goals. And lastly, qualified teachers should be sought out if the parents have inadequate skills to teach the subject to their children. Music is so important to our lives and to the world that the education of this concept must be given the same priority and importance as learning to read and write. It should not be looked at as an elective, but rather as a foundational class with lifelong applications.

MUSIC IS SPIRITUAL

Music is simple, yet at the same time extremely complex. The number of musical combinations of notes, concepts, instruments, voices, styles, and rhythms seem endless. It never ceases to amaze me how many thousands of different melodies were written using the same set of notes! But it shouldn't. Our eternal God, who was and is and is to come, created the expression of music for His glory and from His glory. In His creativity He planned for limitless opportunities and varieties of music to be made. The animals, the birds, the trees, the wind, the oceans, the fish, the mountains, fire, mankind, and even the rocks cry out with music—that is, some form of created sound.

Music Created

God created everything by the sound of His voice. On the first day of creation, "God said, 'Let there be light,' and there was light. God saw that the light was good" (Genesis 1:3-4). At that moment the instantaneous creativity of God birthed music. Light is composed of a variety of waves referred to as the electromagnetic spectrum. In this instance, God spoke both light and sound into existence in our world. The science of sound is foundational to the study of musical ideas and concepts. Adam was able to speak, sing, whistle, clap, stomp, hum, and dance. All of these are basic sound and music concepts that are used to teach beginning music. The birds sang melodies in the skies, the whales sent song signals to their young under the water, the crickets chirped their melody in the evening twilight, the bat listened for a sound echo to set its flying path, and many other animals made their own music unto their God in the created state of our world. When God said, "Let there be light," music in our world began, and it was good!

The Eternal Purpose of Music

Wanted: Musicians and Singers for Timeless Events

The mission of the Christian parent should include training and preparing musicians for the kingdom of God! This does not mean that our children should be professional performers by earthly standards, but rather equipped, prepared music-makers by heavenly standards.

The Musical Universe

In 1772 Johann Bode, a German astronomer, measured the distance between the planets. His mathematical formula was so precise that it later became known as Bode's Law. He stated that all of the planets possessed mean orbital distances from Mercury, which become progressively greater as the planets' distance from the sun increases. The resulting ratio means that each planet vibrates twice as fast as its predecessor and produces a sound with a pitch one octave higher than the previous planet. This ratio is the same as that of the musical tones in an octave, suggesting that the planets themselves form a chain of octaves, with each planet representing one octave. Approximately every twelve years the planets become somewhat aligned with one another. If we could hear the combination of these various tones at this time, they would most likely sound like a musical chord. (See *Good Music, Brighter Children* by Sharlene Habermeyer, Prima Publishing, 1999.) How awesome to think that God has created enormous musical instruments resounding throughout the universe. Could there be other galaxies making music that will need overseers in eternity?

Musical Bodies

We were created with a pulse that keeps a steady and regular beat throughout our lifetime. Without that steady pulse we would become very sick or could even die. That pulse keeps the life-giving blood flowing through every part of our body. Did you ever think of your heart as the first musical instrument that God gave you? The heart keeps a steady beat that allows all other members of our body to function correctly and in unison. God thought this was so important that He gave each of us our own personal, steady beat while still inside our mother's womb. In less than four weeks from conception a little beat-keeper begins to thump a distinct rhythmic pattern similar to the mother's heartbeat. The little baby begins to move his arms, legs, and body to the beat of the music he hears and feels inside his mom.

Music in Scripture

If you were asked whether the Bible says anything about music, you would probably say yes. Many, many Scriptures refer to music, instruments, singing, and joyful sounds. Psalm 150 is a musical passage ending with the exhortation that everything that has breath is to praise the Lord. A favorite music passage of mine is Ephesians 5:18-19, "Be filled with the Spirit; speaking to yourselves in psalms and hymns and spiritual songs, singing and making melody in your heart to the Lord" (KJV). This does not appear to be a suggestion, but rather a command to include music in your life all the time.

Consider also the Scriptures that are not so "musically clear," yet point to musical concepts that show that God filled His Word with ideas about music long before our composers and musicians named the ideas. In Exodus 28:31-35 the priests were instructed to wear long robes trimmed with bells and pomegranates so the bystanders outside the Holy Place could hear the priest walking around inside the holy area. If that music stopped, the now-dead priest would be pulled out of the Temple by a rope that had been previously secured to his leg. The bells and pomegranates represent our modern percussion instruments. God breathed into someone the idea that music or sound could be made for life-giving purposes by striking pomegranates against a bell-type object. That sound meant life to the priest and to those who waited for him outside the inner chamber.

Exodus 19:16-19 records three other musical ideas. First, there was thunder and lightning in the morning and a very loud trumpet blast that filled the camp. Today's musical notation would record these sounds as forte, meaning loud. God is pictured as having a voice of thunder. What does that mean? Well, if you listen closely to the sound of thunder, you would probably describe it as loud, strong, low, and containing stronger and weaker booms. In musical terms you would be able to identify forte (meaning loud), bass (meaning low pitches or tones), and accent marks (certain beats get a stronger emphasis than others). You could say that God sings bass! He has low, deep tones penetrating deep inside our being. Lastly, the sound of the trumpet became louder and louder. This is called a crescendo, music (sounds) that gradually or increasingly become louder.

Many other Scriptures also point to musical concepts and ideas. Numerous instruments are named with specific purposes and assignments. Singing is probably one of the most elementary musical skills that fills the pages of God's Word. The angels sing, and yes, there will be singing in heaven. What part will you be prepared to sing? God filled His Word with music to instruct us how to be musical.

MUSIC IS FUN

I remember, at various stages of my educational process, sitting in classes that seemed rather boring and asking, "What am I ever going to do with this information? Will I ever use it when I grow up?" I sat through several years of private piano lessons and practiced at home on a regular basis (thanks to my mom who insisted that I practice) wondering what good this was going to be for me. And then it began to happen. My elementary music teachers began to ask me to play the piano for school music programs. In junior high school the choir directors used me as one of only a select few regular accompanists. Some of the best times in high school were a direct result of my ability to play the piano. I was able to perform in several musicals, accompany countless choir performances, attend solo and ensemble competitions as a participant and as an accompanist, play a variety of keyboards in several popular/rock concerts, plus participate in many other musical opportunities that came up at church including some travel as part of ministry groups and playing praise and worship for local crusades. These activities made piano fun and worth all the practice. Music has had practical application, meaning, and purpose in my life. I had a skill that made me feel good about myself. Later on I became a private piano teacher and am now able to help other students develop a skill that has become so important to me.

MUSIC HAS EDUCATIONAL VALUE

You will find there are many ways for musical skills to be put to good use. Scholarships is one. My daughter's desire is to become a doctor (that means medical school, and that costs lots of money!). It is very reasonable to expect that she can earn musical scholarships for the purpose of completing her degree. This does not mean she will have to attend a music school and become a musician, but her musical abilities can pay the way for her other goals and desires. Here are some musical educational facts to consider:

Ninety percent of students who participate in their high school band, chorus, and/or orchestra go on to college and complete their undergraduate degree.

Students with band and/or orchestra experience attend college at a rate twice the national average.

Music students outperform non-music students on achievement tests in reading and math. Because of music, their skills in reading, anticipating, memory, listening, forecasting, recall, and concentration are better.

On average, high school music students have higher grade point averages than non-music students in the same school.

Investing in music early is probably better than putting money in the bank for your child's education. With the enhanced IQ and study habits found in many music students, more scholarship money is available.

MUSIC IS A LIFE SKILL

Many say, "I wish I had never stopped taking music lessons!" or "If only I had continued music lessons, I could do this or that." You rarely, if ever, hear an adult say, "Oh, I wish I had stopped taking music lessons!" Many people wish they could go back and start music lessons or that they had continued the music lessons they were taking. Too often adults wish they could play an instrument with or for their children or grandchildren, participate in community or church musical activities, or just have fun with music. Many adults do try to take up an instrument well into their adulthood, but though some do succeed, most do not. Their musical knowledge and abilities are limited. The cares and responsibilities of adult life drain the energies that are needed to learn to play an instrument. However, general music appreciation, knowledge, and listening skills can always be developed and improved well into advanced years. Music is known to be therapy, entertainment, relaxation, and energy for countless senior citizens. Music is a skill that will go on forever, from childhood to adulthood and into eternity. It is in our best interest to learn the basic skills of music early, so we can enjoy the gift God created for us and in us.

MUSIC TRAINING

Most parents deal with the question of whether or not they should provide their child with music lessons. The question should be, *when* do you start musical training, not *should* you start musical training. Parents need to train their children in music just as much as in reading, writing, math, and spelling. Music is a foundational skill that can complement and supplement all other areas of study.

The Baby's Music

In God's wisdom and plan He created each of us with a musical instrument—our heart. Rhythm has begun in every baby. A steady beat begins to play. Music expressions may change throughout the course of our lives, but that inborn music will always be there begging for an opportunity to articulate itself. Many expectant mothers spend time listening to music, or rather having their unborn children listen to music in the womb. Childbirth centers often suggest that laboring mothers listen to music to help them control their pain and deal with the delivery. From there almost every nursery has a music box, a musical mobile hanging from the crib, a Mozart or other lullaby recording, toys that play a tune, or something that makes musical sounds. Moms will sit for hours rocking and singing to their baby, and the baby hasn't even talked or walked—but he has cooed.

If you listen closely you could even call it humming. Babies respond positively to a variety of music-makers. You have already started music lessons, and you probably didn't realize it. Yes, that infant child is processing all those sounds and is forming his own opinion of the musical world.

Young Children and Music

As your child grows into his preschool years, you begin to think about musical experiences in the form of lessons. Remember that some children learn to swim in their mother's arms at birth, and others wait until about three years old and go into the water without Mom. Others wait until about five years old when the mom/child separation issue is not such a concern. But in each case you probably gave your child a bath, and he or she knows what water is and what it feels like. Since you have been providing a variety of musical experiences to your child from birth, your preschooler will already know some things about music; so it is now a matter of choosing a formal avenue of further education for him or her. Many early childhood music programs can provide an excellent foundational exposure to music concepts. There are national businesses that provide music programs, a variety of preschool group music classes available through recreation, community, preschool, and church programs, and private lessons with individual instruction from a teacher. The many theories and words of wisdom available can help you decide when it is best for your child to start formal music lessons. Please refer to the list of resources at the end of the chapter to gather detailed information on this subject.

CHOOSING THE INSTRUMENT

There are many factors to consider when selecting an instrument for your child to play including the cost, the convenience, the room in your house, the musical experiences to achieve, and your goals. Some instruments are less expensive than others. They can be purchased outright or rented with an option to buy. Some instruments are easier to transport than others, and this should be considered in the case of band or orchestra instruments. Let's face it—there are instruments that need a lot of space to set up and learn to play correctly, or they just need room, as in the case of a piano, while other instruments can be packed in a small case and put in a closet for storage. Also be sure to review your child's music goals when deciding on instruments. Look at items that best meet those goals.

Start with the Piano

Learning to play the piano will teach your child all kinds of musical concepts that will be applicable to hundreds of other musical experiences and instruments. The piano is tricky. Your child will learn to use two hands, ten fingers, read music in two different clefs at the same time, listen to what he plays, make his hands and fingers move in different directions, and all kinds of other things. It is a foundational music experience to play the piano. So much of what is learned applies to other instruments, and many other instruments will be so much easier to play after the piano. If your child expresses an intense interest in another instrument, have him or her take about two years of piano first and then go to the other instrument, remembering there are always exceptions to the rules.

I tried to teach my daughter Andrea to play the piano when she was five years old. We worked on and off for almost three years, basically accomplishing nothing. She knew some notes, could read some music, and could play a few one-handed tunes, but I was not pleased with her progress. She kept asking me for a flute. When she was four years old, her part-time preschool teacher brought her own flute into class and played for the children. I did not realize what an impression that made on Andrea. I gave in and bought (not rented) a flute for her when she was eight years old. I found a homeschooled high school student who agreed to teach my daughter. At the end of six weeks not only could she play the flute well enough to participate in the spring homeschool band concert, she sat down and played the piano—with both hands, more difficult music than she left off with about a year earlier. Now almost four years later Andrea not only can play the flute and piano, she has added the viola to her assortment of instruments. Something clicked inside her brain, and it just all came together. Although the piano is the suggested beginning instrument, be sensitive to your child's desires. He or she may know best.

Try a Variety of Instruments

If you start young enough, it is possible for your child to test-play several instruments over the course of five to seven years. Let him or her explore as many as you both feel comfortable with, and then by the time he or she reaches eighth or ninth grade choose one or two instruments to study consistently throughout his or her high school years. He or she will thank you for such a musically diversified experience.

Practice, Practice, Practice

Let's face it, my children did not learn to swim in one day. It took many seasons and repeated effort and instruction. They needed to learn to breathe, then kick, then arm motions, then floating, and on it goes. Learning an instrument requires the same kind of repetition. First you learn steps that are unique to the individual instrument, then the notes, some fingering, technique, and on it goes. A student must work at putting all the elements together to play an instrument. Although it does happen occasionally that a child picks up an instrument and plays it with no lessons or formal training, that is the rare exception and not the rule. Music is a skill that can be taught and can be learned. It will only get better as the ideas and concepts are repeated and perfected.

If the music you are working on comes so easily that you do not have to practice it, then get something harder to work on. Be challenged. Elementary students need at least thirty minutes of playing time per day all week. This can include specific listening time also. I encourage my students to spend Sunday playing the things that they like and know well just for the fun and accomplishment of playing. The other days need to be spent on learning new music, skills, and techniques. Remind your child that his or her teacher will know if he or she has practiced or not. It is not usually possible to fool the teacher!

MUSIC EXPOSURE

The key word to formal musical training is *exposure*. Consistently expose your child as early as you can to every possible music experience that comes to mind. We already pointed out so many things that happen at birth and as an infant. From there, play with your children in musical ways. Sing to them, clap with them, dance with them, or make musical instruments from wooden spoons or pots and pans. Play lots of music around the house, in the car, before bed, anywhere at any time. Expose your child to a variety of styles and kinds of music. Be sure to include vocal music as well as instrumental. Expose your child to concerts. Take them to a music store, and expose them to instruments and rows of sheet music. Take a walk in the park, and expose them to singing birds and chirping crickets—music abounds in nature. Read musical stories and books. Read about composers and hymn-writers. View musical videos during family time. Make lists of places that play music. Make lists of things that make music. Make lists of places where you can hear music. Make a conscious effort to expose your children to music in all its forms and varieties.

MUSIC GOALS

When I made the decision to have all of my children take swimming lessons, I was not planning to train world-champion Gold Medal swimmers. My goal was to train them in an activity that was fun and good for their physical bodies, would build their self-esteem, and would provide an outlet to enjoy God's creation. They could use it all of their lives, not just for a season, and that could possibly save their lives or the life of someone else. For my children, my music goals are very similar. Music is fun. It requires physical coordination. It builds self-esteem. It provides an avenue of praise and worship to God. They can use the skill all of their life, and yes, it could be a venue of saving someone else's eternal life.

Many careers come from a music background. Teachers, performers, composers, directors, moviemakers, radio personnel, recording artists, music therapists, instrument salespersons, instrument construction staff, multimedia and computer personnel, and many others began with music training. Trained and degreed musicians will easily be able to find a variety of well-paying jobs.

So it is important that you and your child take a good look at why you want to study music and an instrument. Ask yourself and your student lots of questions about his or her goals, desires, and talents. Not all music students will have professional music careers, nor do they even want them. Yet music training can supplement and complement the other areas of learning in their life. Some students have only top musical performance and careers in mind; so they need the best teachers, instruments, and resources. Examine your goals carefully because they will be key factors in determining what kind of musical life and education you will pursue for your children.

MUSIC TEACHERS

The art of finding a private music teacher is about as subjective as choosing a color to paint the living room. One person says it must be green, and the next feels it must be blue. Are they both wrong? Are they both right? It is better to outline the parameters of choosing the best color for the dynamics of the room. Does it face a window? Does it get sunlight? What color is the carpet? What is the room size? What is the purpose of the room? Will there be lots of activity, people, and events here, or will it be a quiet place of refuge? How will you paint the room? Will you spray it or use a brush? Will you experiment with a new texturing technique? The decision has been made to begin formal music lessons, but what teacher will you choose?

Teacher Qualifications and Styles

When choosing a teacher, first keep in mind the goals of your child as well as yourself. What do you want from this musical experience? Are you planning to study professionally or casually? Especially with young children, the beginning formal lessons need to be a fun and engaging experience that will inspire the child to continue training. Get off to a good start.

Let's say that you and your child decide that the "room" must be professionally decorated and designed as if it is part of the White House. Then you must seek out professionally trained and degreed musicians who are capable of teaching music at an above-average level. Yet, there are some highly skilled musicians that are not good teachers. Teachers must be accurate in their knowledge and skill, but they also must be able to communicate in a manner that will impact the student toward positive results. I remember when we were looking for a violin teacher for my daughter, Diana. I was given a name of someone who was highly recommended, and I made an appointment with the teacher. At the first lesson, which was held at a local music store, we were escorted into a small (maybe 6 x 5) room, more appropriately called a closet. As the teacher began her explanations of how to hold and care for the violin, I could tell she was well-educated. She was confident and firm in all of her directions. She proceeded to give Diana her assignments for the week, but she was forgetting that my girl was only six; her delivery was directed to a ten-year-old at the very least.

I helped Diana practice as the days went by. However, by the third week she begged me not to take her back to violin lessons. I explained that the teacher was quite competent, well-educated, and a gifted player. This made no difference to Diana. You see, Diana has a very quiet, gentle, and soft spirit. She needed someone to be gentle toward her and not "bark" out the instructions as if she were in the army, even if they were good and correct instructions! As good as this teacher was, I realized that the relationship would never work because the personalities simply did not work well together. I asked Diana not to give up until I could find her a teacher who she felt was kinder and gentler. I finally found another teacher who played well, who did not have as much teaching experience, but who was wonderful with Diana. The lessons were conducted in a spacious, well-lit, decorated basement of a comfortable private home in a pleasant residential area. She and Diana just "clicked" together. Although Diana is very shy and spoke very little, she absorbed everything she was taught and worked cheerfully. It was a good fit.

Evaluate what qualifications are best suited to your goals. If your child is to become a professional musician or performer you need to seek out a highly educated, firm, and technical person to teach him or her. For other musical goals you can probably do very well with a person who is nominally trained, has a heart for teaching and a love of music, and can teach your child to play an instrument or to sing a melody well. One will take every musical detail very seriously, and the other will be less rigid. Both kinds of teachers have their place in the musical world.

Teaching Methods

Like any industry, music has its own theories and approaches to accomplish goals. There are several methods to teach various kinds of learners. Some teachers prefer to train the ear to hear music without reading the music. Others insist on teaching the notes right from the beginning and having the child read what he plays. There are methods that incorporate movement, dance, and related activities to provide a broader range of music exposure. I personally believe balance is the key. Expose your child to various approaches and methods that provide a wide range of experiences. *Be wary of the teacher who says there is only one way or method to teach or train the child in music.* Each child is unique, and so is the method for that child. Be sure to refer to the list of resources at the end of the chapter for further detailed information.

Finding a Teacher

Probably the best source for finding a teacher is a referral from a trusted friend. Many times these teachers do not advertise much because their waiting lists are already long. However, if you need to look elsewhere, various musician associations provide names of teachers. Check with local music stores. They will have these names and phone numbers along with other local private teachers. Check with your local school system's music departments. Many schoolteachers also teach private music lessons after school. Band and orchestra teachers often teach privately or have lists of teachers available to refer to you. Check to see if your city has a band, orchestra, or symphony. Quite often those musicians will teach private lessons. In cities where military bases exist, there may be a military band whose members may offer lessons. Also check at your church or other local churches, especially ones that have large music programs. Ask for the music directors, and then ask for names of those who may be teaching lessons. Check with your homeschool support group, and check classifieds in newsletters. Sometimes you need to call several names before you get a teacher you really want.

Teaching Environment

I took my daughter to a private house to interview a potential teacher. When we arrived, we were escorted to the lowest level of the house into an 8 x 8 windowless, back corner room. The area was set up with keyboards, computers, and shelves with various musical equipment. I learned that the man was divorced and was doing extra teaching to make money (which many private teachers do). However, this environment was a red flag to me. I was not comfortable leaving my daughter in this room where there was no one else around to keep an eye on what was going on. As a private piano teacher and the mother of four children, I teach my lessons in my bright living room while my children are in nearby rooms. It is easy to see what is going on around us, and there is no chance of any improprieties. Be careful to pick an environment that is personally safe, well-lit, warm, and inviting.

Lesson Costs

Check around and try to obtain at least three price quotes of comparable teachers. Check with your local music store to obtain rates from their teachers. They will usually have a variety of rates that match the instruments, time of lessons, and education of the teacher. Try to compare apples to apples with your needs and goals. Young college students will often charge less than more mature and seasoned teachers, but the beginning results could still be very good.

Music lessons are one of the best gifts that grandparents and other relatives can give your children. We have been blessed with in-laws who paid for our instrument rentals. I explained to them the importance of music, our shortage of money, and the many times wasted money is spent on toys and knickknacks that end up in the garbage. Grandma now felt that she had an important part in her grandchild's education, and a great need was met at the same time. Thank you, Grandma!

Lesson Scheduling and Convenience

Children who attend school need after-school lesson scheduling, which can be difficult to find. There are only so many hours that a teacher can teach after school and before bedtime. Homeschooled students have the flexibility of taking lessons during the daytime hours and should be careful not to take time slots away from schooled children.

In a well-populated area it should not be necessary to drive over ten miles to find a good teacher, especially at beginning levels. If your child has reached top performance levels and wants to pursue scholarships and more elite training, you may want to consider driving farther to find a highly qualified teacher to help meet those goals.

Recitals and Performances

The primary reason for recitals is to provide opportunities for your child to play in front of other people. While this is a very good experience for some, for others it can mean the difference between continuing lessons or not. Some children just cannot handle performance in front of others. Consider having a private recital with close friends and family in the comfort of your own home. Invite your instrument teacher, and just have fun.

There will be plenty of time for onstage performances if that is part of your child's goals.

On the other hand, some students thrive on being able to perform in front of strangers. It builds their confidence and pushes them to higher levels of playing. It also prepares them for future performance opportunities. These students need all the playing opportunities that you can find for them. You may even want to consider community symphonies, bands, orchestras, or choirs for further exposure.

Remember that recitals and performances take time. These are more events to schedule into your life. Many homeschoolers have the tendency to overcommit their time and energy. If you choose to incorporate these activities into your music education, be sure to allow enough time to make the experience a good one.

It is not a bad idea to change teachers at least once and maybe twice during your child's instrumental music training. Different teachers can provide different perspectives, ideas, and styles that can enrich the musical experience. I know that I changed teachers when I entered junior high school. I found that one of the music school teachers could teach me styles and techniques that I was not previously exposed to, and that allowed me to play for shows and concerts throughout my high school years. Be careful not to change teachers every year unless there is a good reason such as a geographical move or death. Honor the teacher to whom you have committed. Be on time, pay the fees as agreed, and monitor your child's practice.

It is impossible to live one day without the sounds of music in your ear. The sounds of nature and animals, the rhythms of machines and tools, the beats of clocks and hearts, the patterns of letters and shapes all point to a created phenomenon called music. Music is one of the greatest, if not the greatest, expressions of our being. Music is eternal. It will fill the expanses of time and space. It is the avenue of worship unto our God. It is our responsibility to know and understand the basic foundations of this concept just as with our other homeschooled subjects. Music is fun, it is exciting, it is useful, it is eternal, it is life!

Laurinda Curti is a licensed Kindermusik Educator. She teaches home-school students ages five through twelve general music classes as part of High Country Enrichment Classes at New Life Church. She runs her own private piano studio, where she specializes in foundational music skills. Laurinda and her husband, George, have four children and reside in Colorado Springs, Colorado, where they attend New Life Church. She currently homeschools three of her children, and they are all actively pursuing musical training.

Resources

Books

Raising Musical Kids, A Guide for Parents by Robert A. Cutietta (Oxford University Press, 2001).

How to Grow a Young Music Lover by Cheri Fuller (Harold Shaw, 1994).

Good Music, Brighter Children by Sharlene Habermeyer (Prima Publishing, 1999).

Sound of Heaven, Symphony of Earth by Ray Hughes (Morning Star, 2000).

Spiritual Moments with the Great Composers by Patrick Kavanaugh (Zondervan, 1995).

Making Music with Your Child by Kia Portafekas (MMB Music, Inc., 2001).

The Big Book of Music Games by Debra Olson Pressnall (Instructional Fair, 1998).

A Parent's Guide to Teaching Music by Jim Probasco (Betterway Publications, Inc., 1992).

The I Can't Sing Book for Grownups Who Can't Carry a Tune in a Paper Bag by Jackie Silberb (Gryphon House, 1999).

Music Catalogs

Friendship House
29313 Clemens Road #2-G
P.O. Box 450978
Cleveland, Ohio 44145-0623
1-800-791-9846
www.friendshiphouse.com

Music in Motion
P.O. Box 833814
Richardson, TX 75083-3814
1-800-445-0649
www.musicmotion.com

Young Musicians, Inc.
P.O. Box 48036
Fort Worth, TX 76148
1-800-826-8648
www.ymonlin.com

Appendix I

STATE BY STATE
TESTING INFORMATION

ALABAMA

 Test: Stanford Achievement Test (SAT), 9th edition.

ALASKA

 Test: California Achievement Test (CAT), 5th edition.

ARIZONA

 Test: Stanford Achievement Test (SAT), 9th edition.

ARKANSAS

 Test: Stanford Achievement Test (SAT), 9th edition, complete battery.
 Subjects tested: math, reading/language arts, social studies, science.
 Grade level: 5, 7, 10.
 Test: Criterion-referenced test.
 Subjects tested: math, English, reading, writing.
 Grade level: 4, 8, 11, 12.

CALIFORNIA

 Test: Stanford Achievement Test (SAT), 9th edition.
 Subjects tested: reading/language arts, math.
 Grade level: 2, 3, 4, 5, 6, 7, 8.
 Test: Statewide standards-based assessment being developed.

COLORADO

 Test: Colorado Student Assessment Program (CSAP) developed in-state to match statewide curriculum frameworks.

CONNECTICUT

Test: Connecticut Mastery Test (state-developed).
Grade level: 4, 6, 8.

DELAWARE

Test: Delaware State Testing Program (DSTP)—standards-based, developed in-state.
Subjects tested: English/language arts, math.
Grade level: 3, 5, 8, 10.
Subjects tested: science, social studies.
Grade level: 4, 6, 8, 11.

FLORIDA

Test: Florida Comprehensive Achievement Test (FCAT)—developed for Florida by CTB/McGraw Hill to reflect state curriculum standards.
Test: Each district chooses its own norm-referenced test; tests in use include California Achievement Test, Stanford Achievement Test, National Achievement Test, Iowa Test of Basic Skills, others.

GEORGIA

Test: Georgia Kindergarten Assessment Program (GKAP)—state-developed.
Grade level: Rising kindergarten students.
Test: Iowa Test of Basic Skills (ITBS).
Subjects tested: reading, math.
Grade level: 3, 5, 8.

HAWAII

Test: Statewide assessment system.
Grade level: 3, 6, 8.

IDAHO

Test: Iowa Test of Basic Skills (ITBS).

ILLINOIS

Test: Illinois Goal Assessment Program (IGAP).
Subjects tested: reading, math, writing.
Grade level: 3, 6, 8, 10.
Subjects tested: Science, social studies.

Grade level: 4, 7, 11.

INDIANA

Test: Indiana Statewide Testing for Educational Progress (ISTEP)—developed to meet Indiana state standards by CTB/McGraw Hill.
Subjects tested: reading/language arts, math.
Grade level: 3, 6, 8, 10.

IOWA

Test: Iowa does not currently have a compulsory statewide assessment program, though the Iowa Test of Basic Skills (ITBS) is available to all schools on a voluntary basis.

KANSAS

Test: State-developed assessment tests, standards-based.
Subjects tested: reading.
Grade level: 3, 7, 10.
Subjects tested: writing, science.
Grade level: 5, 8, 10.
Subjects tested: math.
Grade level: 4, 7, 10.
Subjects tested: social studies.
Grade level: 5, 8, 11.

KENTUCKY

Test: Kentucky Instructional Results Information Systems (KIRIS).
Subjects tested: science, social studies, math, reading, arts/humanities, practical living/vocational studies.
Grade level: 4, 8, 11.

LOUISIANA

Test: California Achievement Test (CAT).
Subjects tested: reading/language arts, math.
Grade level: 4.
Test: Louisiana Educational Assessment Program (LEAP).
Subjects tested: language arts, math.
Grade level: 3.
Test: Statewide standards-based assessment program being developed.

MAINE

Test: Maine Educational Assessment.

Subjects tested: reading, writing, math, science, social studies, arts and humanities.

Grade level: 4, 8, 11.

Subjects tested: Health.

Grade level: 4, 8.

MARYLAND

Test: Maryland School Performance Assessment Program (MSPAP).

Subjects tested: reading, math, English/language arts, science, social studies.

Grade level: 3, 5, 8, 11.

MASSACHUSETTS

Test: Massachusetts Educational Assessment Program.

Subjects tested: English/language arts, math, science/technology, history, and social science.

Grade level: 4, 8, 10.

MICHIGAN

Test: Michigan Educational Assessment Program (MEAP).

Subjects tested: math, reading.

Grade level: 4, 7.

Subjects tested: science, writing.

Grade level: 5, 8.

MINNESOTA

Test: Minnesota Comprehensive Assessment Program.

Subjects tested: reading, math.

Grade level: 3, 5, 8-12.

Subjects tested: writing.

Grade level: 5.

MISSISSIPPI

Test: Iowa Test of Basic Skills (ITBS).

Subjects tested: reading/language arts, math.

Grade level: 4, 5, 6, 7, 8, 9.

Test: Iowa Test of Basic Skills/Iowa Test of Achievement and Proficiency (combined).
Grade level: 9.

MISSOURI

Test: Missouri Assessment Program (MAP)—replaces the Missouri Mastery and Achievement Test program; MAP is being developed by the state in conjunction with CTB/McGraw Hill.
Subjects tested: math.
Grade level: 4, 8, 10.
Subjects tested: English.
Grade level: 3, 7, 11.
Subjects tested: science.
Grade level: 3, 7, 11.
Subjects tested: social studies.
Grade level: 4, 8, 11.

MONTANA

Test: Districts can choose from among commercially prepared tests.
Subjects tested: math, reading, other "core subjects."
Grade level: 4, 8, 10.

NEBRASKA

Test: Nebraska does not currently have a statewide assessment program.

NEVADA

Test: Districts can choose from among commercially prepared tests.
Subjects tested: reading, writing, math.
Grade level: 4, 8, 11.

NEW HAMPSHIRE

Test: New Hampshire Educational Improvement and Assessment Program (NHEIAP).
Subjects tested: English/language arts, math.
Grade level: 3.
Subjects tested: English/language arts, math, science, social studies.
Grade level: 6, 10.

NEW JERSEY

Test: Elementary School Proficiency Test (ESPA).
Grade level: 4.

NEW YORK

Test: Pupil Evaluation Program (PEP).
Subjects tested: reading, math.
Grade level: 3, 6.
Subjects tested: writing.
Grade level: 5.
Test: Program Evaluation Test (PET).
Subjects tested: science.
Grade level: 3-8.
Subjects tested: social studies.
Grade level: 6, 8.
Test: New standards-based tests are in development.

NORTH CAROLINA

Test: North Carolina End of Grade Test.
Subjects tested: reading, math.
Grade level: 3-8.
Test: North Carolina Developed Open-Ended Written (essay) Test.
Subjects tested: reading, math.
Grade level: 4, 8.

NORTH DAKOTA

Test: CTBS, Fifth Edition: Terra Nova, and companion test: Test of
Cognitive Skills, 2nd Edition.
Subjects tested: Multi-Subject Battery Test.
Grade level: 4, 6, 8, 10.

OHIO

Test: Ohio Proficiency Test.
Subjects tested: reading, writing, math, science, citizenship.
Grade level: 4, 6, 9, 12.

OKLAHOMA

Test: Iowa Test of Basic Skills (ITBS).
Grade level: 3, 7.

Test: Oklahoma Core Curriculum Tests.
Subjects tested: math, science, reading, history, writing.
Grade level: 5, 8, 11.

OREGON

Test: State-developed, criterion-referenced tests.
Subjects tested: writing.
Grade level: 5, 8, 10.
Subjects tested: reading and literature, math.
Grade level: 3, 5, 8, 10.

PENNSYLVANIA

Test: Pennsylvania System of School Assessment.
Subjects tested: reading.
Grade level: 5, 8, 11.
Subjects tested: writing.
Grade level: 6, 9.
Subjects tested: math.
Grade level: 5, 8, 11.

RHODE ISLAND

Test: Metropolitan Achievement Test.
Grade level: 4, 8.
Test: Rhode Island Writing Test.
Grade level: 3, 7, 10.
Test: New Standards.
Subjects tested: math.
Grade level: 4, 8, 10.
Subjects tested: English/language arts.
Grade level: 4, 8.
Test: Health Education Assessment.
Grade level: 5, 9.

SOUTH CAROLINA

Test: South Carolina Basic Skills Assessment Program (BSAP).
Grade level: 3, 6, 8, 10.
Test: Metropolitan Achievement Test, seventh edition (MAT7).
Subjects tested: language arts.
Grade level: 4, 5, 7, 9, 11.

SOUTH DAKOTA

Test: Nationally standardized, norm-referenced achievement and ability test.
Subjects tested: reading, math.
Grade level: 2, 4, 8, 11.
Subjects tested: writing achievement.
Grade level: 5, 9.

TENNESSEE

Test: Terra Nova, Complete Battery Plus.
Subjects tested: reading/language arts, math, science, social studies.
Grade level: 3, 4, 5, 6, 7, 8.

TEXAS

Test: Texas Assessment of Academic Skills (TAAS).
Subjects tested: reading, math.
Grade level: 3, 4, 5, 6, 7, 8, 10.
Subjects tested: writing.
Grade level: 4, 8.
Subjects tested: social studies, science.
Grade level: 8.

UTAH

Test: Stanford Achievement Test (SAT), 9th edition.
Grade level: 5, 8, 11.

VERMONT

Test: Vermont Comprehensive Assessment System (VCAS).
Subjects tested: early reading.
Grade level: 2.
Subjects tested: math, English/language arts.
Grade level: 4, 8, 10.
Subjects tested: science.
Grade level: 6, 11.
Subjects tested: history, social studies, geography.
Grade level: 6, 9, 11.
Test: Local districts choose a norm-referenced test (not mandatory).
Grade level: 5, 9, 11.

VIRGINIA

Test: Stanford Achievement Test (SAT), 9th edition, Form TA.

Subjects tested: reading/language arts, math (science and social studies optional).

Grade level: 4, 6, 9.

Test: Virginia Standards of Learning (SOL) Test.

Subjects tested: English, math, science, social studies.

Grade level: 3.

Subjects tested: English, math, science, social studies, computer technology.

Grade level: 5.

Subjects tested: English, math, science, social studies, computer technology.

Grade level: 8.

WASHINGTON

Test: Comprehensive Test of Basic Skills (CTBS).

Grade level: Kindergarten.

Test: Statewide Assessment Program tests.

Subjects tested: reading, math, language, listening.

Grade level: 1, 2.

Subjects tested: listening.

Grade level: 3, 4, 5, 6, 7, 8.

Subjects tested: reading/language arts, spelling, math, science, social sciences.

Grade level: 3, 4, 5, 6, 7, 8, 9, 10, 11.

WISCONSIN

Test: Terra Nova.

Grade level: 4, 8, 10.

Test: Wisconsin Reading Comprehension Test.

Grade level: 3.

Note: Many states are in the midst of developing their own state standards tests. This list is subject to change. Check with your state's testing requirements at their department of education's website for updates.

Appendix II

LEARNING
STYLES INVENTORY

Below you will find a checklist found in *Success in School: Building on Biblical Principles* by Vicki Caruana (Bemidji, MN: Focus Publishing, 2000).

LINGUISTIC INTELLIGENCE

__ writes better than average for age.
__ spins tall tales or tells jokes and stories.
__ has a good memory for names, places, dates, or trivia.
__ enjoys word games.
__ enjoys reading books.
__ spells words accurately.
__ appreciates nonsense rhymes, puns, tongue twisters, etc.
__ has a good vocabulary for age.
__ communicates to others in a highly verbal manner.

LOGICAL-MATHEMATICAL INTELLIGENCE

__ asks a lot of questions about how things work.
__ computes arithmetic problems in his/her head quickly.
__ enjoys math class.
__ finds math computer games interesting.
__ enjoys playing chess, checkers, or other strategy games.
__ enjoys putting things in categories or hierarchies.
__ likes to experiment in a way that shows higher-order cognitive thinking processes.
__ thinks on a more abstract or conceptual level than peers.
__ has a good sense of cause-effect for age.

SPATIAL INTELLIGENCE

___ reports clear visual images.

___ reads maps, charts, and diagrams more easily than text.

___ daydreams more than peers.

___ enjoys art activities.

___ draws figures that are advanced for age.

___ likes to view movies, slides, or other visual presentations.

___ enjoys doing puzzles, mazes, "Where's Waldo?" or similar visual activities.

___ builds interesting three-dimensional constructions for age.

___ gets more out of pictures than words while reading.

___ doodles on worksheets, workbooks, or other materials.

BODILY-KINESTHETIC INTELLIGENCE

___ excels in one or more sports.

___ moves, twitches, taps, or fidgets while seated for a long time in one spot.

___ cleverly mimics other people's gestures or mannerisms.

___ loves to take things apart and put them back together again.

___ puts his/her hands all over something he/she has just seen.

___ enjoys running, jumping, wrestling, or similar activities.

___ shows skill in a craft.

___ has a dramatic way of expressing herself/himself.

___ reports different physical sensations while thinking or working.

___ enjoys working with clay or other tactile experiences.

MUSICAL INTELLIGENCE

___ tells you when music sounds off-key or disturbing in some other way.

___ remembers melodies of songs.

___ has a good singing voice.

___ plays a musical instrument or sings in a choir or other group.

___ has a rhythmic way of speaking and/or moving.

___ unconsciously hums to himself/herself.

___ taps rhythmically on the table or desk as she/he works.

___ sensitive to environmental noises.

___ responds favorably when a piece of music is put on.

___ sings songs that he/she has learned outside of the classroom.

INTERPERSONAL INTELLIGENCE

__ enjoys socializing with peers.

__ seems to be a natural leader.

__ gives advice to friends who have problems.

__ seems to be street-smart.

__ belongs to clubs, committees, or other organizations.

__ enjoys informally teaching other kids.

__ likes to play games with other kids.

__ has two or more close friends.

__ has a good sense of empathy or concern for others.

__ others seek out his/her company.

INTRAPERSONAL INTELLIGENCE

__ displays a sense of independence or a strong will.

__ has a realistic sense of his/her strengths and weaknesses.

__ does well when left alone to play or study.

__ marches to a beat of a different drummer.

__ has an interest or hobby that he/she doesn't talk much about.

__ prefers working alone.

__ accurately expresses how he/she is feeling.

__ is able to learn from his/her failures and successes in life.

__ has high self-esteem.

Appendix III

SPIRITUAL GIFTS
INVENTORY

"Now concerning spiritual gifts . . ."

Spiritual gifts are God-given abilities which the Holy Spirit gives to each new follower of Christ Jesus. Some of the gifts are designed to help fellow Christians grow towards spiritual maturity. Other gifts are designed to bring the good news of salvation in word and deed to those living within a broken community.

> *"There are different kinds of gifts, but the same Spirit*
> *There are different kinds of service, but the same Lord*
> *There are different kinds of working, but the same God*
> *works all of them in all men . . . for the common good."*
> 1 CORINTHIANS 12:4-7

HOW DO I FIND MY GIFT?

The process of discovering your spiritual gifts includes the following steps. It is important to realize that these are not automatic, and may require years of trial and error, and yet God will "steer" each believer into the area where He wants them to serve.

• Learn about spiritual gifts. Read the passages related to spiritual gifts in Ephesians 4, 1 Peter 4, 1 Corinthians 12, and Romans 12. Read the brochure on gifts written by Ron Ritchie.

• Try a wide variety of ministries.

• Find out which ones you felt were most effective.

• Ask good friends, who have seen you serve, to honestly tell you where they think you're most effective.

• Take a spiritual gifts test. There are a number available and these are not fool-proof, but they often help narrow the options down.

• Ask yourself after a while: what do I really enjoy doing? Surprise! The place where God wants you to serve will be the place that "fits" you the best, and ultimately where you'll find the most fulfillment. If you find yourself dreading a particular ministry, it may be that you're not gifted for it. In fact, some people do not think that their gift is in a certain area, because they like it too much. Serving and using your gifts is meant to be a joy (although it often includes hard work), not a miserable experience.

Once you've found your area of giftedness, look for opportunities to use it! There are usually many needy areas in the church that could use someone like you. If you have a passion for a ministry that doesn't yet exist, then pray about it, seek other like-minded people, and wait for God's timing. It might be that He wants you to wait a year or two, but at the same time it might be a ministry just waiting for someone like you to get it started. But don't be a lone ranger—ministries work best when a team of people with different gifts work together.

FBC SPIRITUAL GIFTS INVENTORY

Respond to each of the statements to follow according to the following scale. Circle your choice.

3 = Consistently, definitely true

2 = Most of the time, usually true

1 = Some of the time, once in a while

0 = Not at all, never

Important note: Answer according to who you are, not who you would like to be or think you ought to be. *How true are these statements of you? To what degree do these statements reflect your usual tendencies?*

0 1 2 3   1. I like to organize people, tasks, and events.

0 1 2 3   2. I would like to start churches in places where they do not presently exist.

0 1 2 3   3. I can readily distinguish between spiritual truth and error, good and evil.

0 1 2 3   4. I tend to see the potential in people.

0 1 2 3   5. I communicate the gospel to others with clarity and effectiveness.

0 1 2 3   6. I find it natural and easy to trust God to answer my prayers.

0 1 2 3   7. I give liberally and joyfully to people in financial need or to projects requiring support.

0 1 2 3   8. I enjoy working behind the scenes to support the work of others.

0 1 2 3   9. I am approached by people who want to know my perspective on a particular biblical truth.

0 1 2 3   10. I am able to motivate others to accomplish a goal.

0 1 2 3   11. I empathize with hurting people and desire to help in their healing process.

0 1 2 3   12. I can speak in a way that results in conviction and change in the lives of others.

0 1 2 3   13. There is great joy in doing little jobs around the church.

0 1 2 3   14. I enjoy spending time nurturing and caring for others.

0 1 2 3   15. I am able to communicate God's word effectively.

0 1 2 3   16. I am often sought out by others for advice about spiritual or personal matters.

0 1 2 3   17. I am careful, thorough, and skilled at managing details.

0 1 2 3   18. I am attracted to the idea of serving in another country or ethnic community.

0 1 2 3   19. I frequently am able to judge a person's character based upon first impressions.

0 1 2 3   20. I enjoy reassuring and strengthening those who are discouraged.

0 1 2 3   21. I consistently look for opportunities to build relationships with non-Christians.

0 1 2 3   22. I have confidence in God's continuing provision and help, even in difficult times.

0 1 2 3   23. I give more than a tithe so that kingdom work can be accomplished.

0 1 2 3   24. I enjoy doing routine tasks that support the ministry.

0 1 2 3   25. I receive information from the Spirit that I did not acquire through natural means.

0 1 2 3   26. I am able to influence others to achieve a vision.

0 1 2 3   27. I can patiently support those going through painful experiences as they try to stabilize their lives.

0 1 2 3   28. I feel responsible to confront others with the truth.

0 1 2 3   29. I enjoy doing routine tasks for the glory of God.

0 1 2 3   30. I have compassion for wandering believers and want to protect them.

0 1 2 3   31. I spend time in study knowing that presenting truth will make a difference in the lives of people.

0 1 2 3   32. I can often find simple, practical solutions in the midst of conflict or confusion.

0 1 2 3   33. I can clarify goals and develop strategies or plans to accomplish them.

0 1 2 3   34. I am willing to take an active part in starting a new church.

0 1 2 3   35. I can see through phoniness or deceit before it is evident to others.

0 1 2 3   36. I give hope to others by directing them to the promises of God.

0 1 2 3   37. I am effective at adapting the gospel message so that it connects with an individual's felt need.

0 1 2 3   38. I believe that God will help me to accomplish great things.

0 1 2 3   39. I manage my money well in order to free more of it for giving.

0 1 2 3   40. I willingly take on a variety of odd jobs around the church to meet the needs of others.

0 1 2 3   41. I genuinely believe the Lord directs strangers to me who need to get connected to others.

0 1 2 3   42. I can adjust my leadership style to bring out the best in others.

0 1 2 3   43. I enjoy helping people sometimes regarded as undeserving or beyond help.

0 1 2 3   44. I boldly expose cultural trends, teaching, or events which contradict biblical principles.

0 1 2 3   45. I receive great satisfaction in doing small or trivial tasks in church.

0 1 2 3   46. I like to provide guidance for the whole person—relationally, emotionally, spiritually, etc.

0 1 2 3   47. I pay close attention to the words, phrases, and meanings of those who teach.

0 1 2 3   48. I can easily select the most effective course of action from among several alternatives.

0 1 2 3   49. I can identify and effectively use the resources needed to accomplish tasks.

0 1 2 3   50. I can adapt well to different cultures and surroundings.

0 1 2 3   51. I tend to see rightness or wrongness in situations.

0 1 2 3   52. I reassure those who need to take courageous action in their faith, family, or life.

0 1 2 3   53. I invite unbelievers to accept Christ as their Savior.

0 1 2 3   54. I trust God in circumstances where success cannot be guaranteed by human effort alone.

0 1 2 3   55. I am challenged to limit my lifestyle in order to give away a higher percentage of my income.

0 1 2 3   56. I see spiritual significance in doing practical tasks.

0 1 2 3   57. I have insight or just know something to be true.

0 1 2 3   58. I set goals and manage people and resources effectively to accomplish them.

0 1 2 3   59. I have great compassion for hurting people.

0 1 2 3   60. I see most actions as right or wrong, and feel the need to correct the wrong.

0 1 2 3   61. I find more satisfaction in doing a job than in finding someone else to do it.

0 1 2 3   62. I can faithfully provide long term support and concern for others.

0 1 2 3   63. I like to take a systematic approach to my study of the Bible.

0 1 2 3   64. I can anticipate the likely consequences of an individual's or group's action.

0 1 2 3   65. I like to help organizations or groups become more efficient.

0 1 2 3   66. I can relate to others in culturally sensitive ways.

0 1 2 3   67. I receive affirmation from others concerning the reliability of my insights or perceptions.

0 1 2 3   68. I strengthen those who are wavering in their faith.

0 1 2 3   69. I openly tell people that I am a Christian and want them to ask me about my faith.

0 1 2 3   70. I am convinced of God's daily presence and action in my life.

0 1 2 3   71. I like knowing that my financial support makes a real difference in the lives of God's people.

0 1 2 3   72. I like to find small things that need to be done and often do them without being asked.

0 1 2 3   73. I have suddenly known some things about others, but did not know how I knew them.

0 1 2 3   74. I influence others to perform to the best of their capability.

0 1 2 3   75. I can look beyond a person's handicap or problems to see a life that matters to God.

0 1 2 3   76. I like people who are honest and will speak the truth.

0 1 2 3   77. I like to do things without attracting much attention.

0 1 2 3   78. I enjoy giving guidance and practical support to a small group of people.

0 1 2 3   79. I can communicate scripture in ways that motivate others to study and want to learn more.

0 1 2 3   80. I can give practical advice to help others through complicated situations.

0 1 2 3   81. I enjoy learning about how organizations function.

0 1 2 3   82. I enjoy pioneering new undertakings.

0 1 2 3   83. I can identify preaching, teaching, or communication which is not true to the Bible.

0 1 2 3   84. I like motivating others to take steps for spiritual growth.

0 1 2 3   85. I openly and confidently tell others about what Christ has done for me.

0 1 2 3   86. I am regularly challenging others to trust God.

0 1 2 3   87. I give generously due to my commitment to stewardship.

0 1 2 3   88. I feel comfortable being a helper, assisting others to do their job more effectively.

0 1 2 3   89. I discover important biblical truths when reading or studying Scripture which benefits others in the body of Christ.

0 1 2 3   90. I am able to cast a vision that others want to be a part of.

0 1 2 3   91. I enjoy bringing hope and joy to people living in difficult circumstances.

0 1 2 3   92. I will speak God's truth, even in places where it is unpopular or difficult for others to accept.

0 1 2 3   93. Others have mentioned that I seem to enjoy routine tasks and that I do them well.

0 1 2 3   94. I can gently restore wandering believers to faith and fellowship.

0 1 2 3   95. I can present information and skills to others at a level that makes it easy for them to grasp and apply to their lives.

0 1 2 3   96. I can apply scriptural truth that others regard as practical and helpful.

0 1 2 3   97. I can visualize a coming event, anticipate potential problems and develop backup plans.

0 1 2 3   98. I am able to orchestrate or oversee several church ministries.

0 1 2 3   99. I can sense when demonic forces are at work in a person or situation.

0 1 2 3   100. I am able to challenge or rebuke others in order to foster spiritual growth.

0 1 2 3   101. I seek opportunities to talk about spiritual matters with unbelievers.

0 1 2 3   102. I can move forward in spite of opposition or lack of support when I sense God's blessing on an undertaking.

0 1 2 3   103. I believe I have been given an abundance of resources so that I can give more to the Lord's work.

0 1 2 3   104. I readily and happily use my natural learned skills to help wherever needed.

0 1 2 3   105. I confidently share my knowledge and insights with others.

0 1 2 3   106. I figure out where we need to go and help others to get there.

0 1 2 3   107. I enjoy doing practical things for others who are in need.

0 1 2 3   108. I feel compelled to expose sin whenever I see it and to challenge people to repentance.

0 1 2 3   109. I prefer being active and doing something rather than talking, reading or listening to a speaker.

0 1 2 3   110. I enjoy patiently but firmly nurturing others in their development as believers.

0 1 2 3   111. I enjoy explaining things to people so that they can grow spiritually and personally.

0 1 2 3   112. I have insights into how to solve problems that others do not see.

SPIRITUAL GIFTS INVENTORY SCORE SHEET

1	2	3	4	5	6	7	8	9	10	11	12	13	14	15	16
17	18	19	20	21	22	23	24	25	26	27	28	29	30	31	32
33	34	35	36	37	38	39	40	41	42	43	44	45	46	47	48
49	50	51	52	53	54	55	56	57	58	59	60	61	62	63	64
65	66	67	68	69	70	71	72	73	74	75	76	77	78	79	80
81	82	83	84	85	86	87	88	89	90	91	92	93	94	95	96
97	98	99	100	101	102	103	104	105	106	107	108	109	110	111	112
A	**B**	**C**	**D**	**E**	**F**	**G**	**H**	**I**	**J**	**K**	**L**	**M**	**N**	**O**	**P**

A = administration   I = knowledge
B = apostleship   J = leadership
C = discernment   K = mercy
D = encouragement   L = prophecy
E = evangelism   M = serving
F = faith   N = shepherding
G = giving   O = teaching
H = helps   P = wisdom

The gifts of *healing, interpretation, miracles* and *tongues* are not included in this *Spiritual Gifts Inventory* only because their presence in the life of a believer tends to be self-evident. God can use them whenever and wherever He chooses.

Used with permission from Fellowship Bible Church, Colorado Springs, Colorado.

INDEX

THE ABC'S OF HOMESCHOOLING

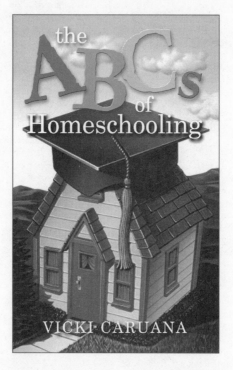

The mothers in her children's play group all attended the same church, had similar interests, and held the same beliefs. Yet when the topic of schooling came up, they had differing ideas that always divided them. Vicki Caruana was the only one choosing to send her children to public school.

Vicki now homeschools—the choice that was furthest from her mind all those years ago—and she writes this book not to convince you that there is only one way to educate a child, but to share with you the stories of why various families have chosen to homeschool.

More moms and dads than ever are now considering homeschooling as an option. But how can parents know if that's the right choice for their kids? To help in that decision, a veteran home educator shares the basics parents need to know about homeschooling, addressing attitudes and assumptions commonly held, and blending in the stories of other families to show the various reasons why they chose that route. In doing so, she enables parents to make an informed decision.

ISBN 1-58134-258-6
$11.99 Trade Paperback

Formerly a public school educator, **Vicki Caruana** frequently speaks at homeschool conventions and leads workshops while also homeschooling her two sons.

THE ORGANIZED HOMESCHOOLER

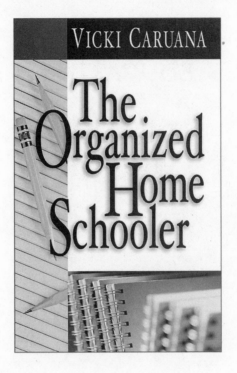

A veteran educator has compiled her most-requested homeschooling workshop material so that families can become more proficient in educating their kids. Covering issues like time management, space usage and materials, Vicki Caruana addresses a variety of organizational needs to help families structure not only their work areas, but also their thinking, their paperwork—and each other! By the book's end, she inspires readers to reevaluate, reorganize, and form new habits, leaving behind the stress and inefficiency of a cluttered life.

Chapter titles include: "Organize Your Thoughts," ". . . Time," ". . . Space," ". . . Supplies and Materials," ". . . Paperwork," ". . . Family," "The Task of Reorganizing," "The Nuts and Bolts of an Organized Homeschool," "A Homeschool File System," and "The List of Lists for Homeschooling."

ISBN 1-58134-305-1
$11.99 Trade Paperback

Formerly a public school educator, **Vicki Caruana** frequently speaks at homeschool conventions and leads workshops while also homeschooling her two sons.

EDUCATING YOUR GIFTED CHILD

Every child is a unique and precious treasure from God. And while each one has been given talents and strengths, some children are obviously more gifted academically. If you've been blessed with one or more gifted children, you know that this joy also raises plenty of questions and concerns. What will keep them challenged and best meet their needs? Will traditional schools suffocate or stimulate their gifts?

Vicki Caruana is able to help you answer these questions and more, thanks to her strong ties in both the gifted education and homeschooling communities. She covers a wide range of topics in-depth, from the characteristics of and myths about gifted kids, to matching teaching and learning styles and handling family dynamics. With stories from her own experiences and those of other parents, advice from experts in the field, and extensive appendices on resources and support groups, she gives you a source of encouragement and guidance in making educational choices for gifted children from preschool-age on up.

ISBN 1-58134-356-6
$13.99 Trade Paperback

Formerly a public school educator, **Vicki Caruana** frequently speaks at homeschool conventions and leads workshops while also homeschooling her two sons.